I0030221

Home Selling

For

Smarties

The Consumer's Insider Guide

By Charles Chaplin
(no kidding)

**Binx
Publishing**

Seattle, WA

Copyright © 2014 by Charles Chaplin

All rights reserved. This book may not be reproduced or used in any manner whatsoever without express written permission of the author except for brief quotations in a book review. Anyone wishing to use this book in an educational venue should contact the author first for written permission and to inquire about bulk orders. To contact the author, please reference the book title in the subject header and send an email to: charles@lifeinseattle.com.

Published by Binx Publishing Seattle, WA

ISBN: 978-0-985210-3-3-5

Cover design, Copyright © 2014 C Square Designs. All rights reserved.

Author Photo, Copyright © 2012 Pete Kaiser. All rights reserved.

Books by Charles Chaplin

Nonfiction

The Smarties Books: The Consumer's Insider Guides

Home Buying For Smarties

Home Selling For Smarties

Fiction

The Alex Campbell Real Estate Mystery Novel Series

No-List Alex (1)

No Serenity (2)

No Rest (3)

Note: these titles can be read in any order.

About This Book...

Whether you are a first time home seller or a repeat home seller, this book will help you organize your home selling process and show you what to watch out for and avoid. It provides you with hands-on, agent-in-the-field information which should help you to make a more informed decision when and if you sell. There are real life stories included which help to illustrate the information and points made. The book is written from a consumer's standpoint.

Since 2004, I have volunteered to teach hundreds of real estate classes, quite a few of them home selling classes. The class is highly rated and everyone learns something, including me. Attendees kept telling me I should put the class information in a book. I listened and here it is! I share my opinions (good and bad) about the industry throughout. As I say at the start of each class that I teach, you won't leave here a real estate expert. Some of what is mentioned will ring true with you and some of it will not. Take what you like and leave the rest; most important, think for yourself. But first, as with everything in business, here is the legal disclaimer. This will be a good trial run for you to read, as it certainly is a preview of what is to come when filling out the listing paperwork!

The Not-so-Fine Print...

This book is intended for informational purposes only, to help home sellers become better informed and educated as to the home selling process before listing. All information (factual or opinion) provided herein is from reliable sources but is not guaranteed. State residential real estate laws and practices vary. Legal terms, real estate terms, rules and regulations, common ways of doing business may change or vary. It is up to the reader to independently investigate, verify and determine any changes and/or variations to the information provided. The "Real Life" sections and personal story examples have been altered to protect the identity of anyone involved.

This book is written from the standpoint of real estate regulations that are currently in place in Washington State, where the author practices. Other state laws and rules may vary. However, the overall information in this book should be helpful to any home owner who is interested in selling within the United States. No legal, real estate, financial, or tax related advice is given or implied. The opinions expressed in this book are the author's and are based on his experience working in the industry and his unique take on the real estate industry. Readers should investigate any issues or opinions expressed in this book on their own and form their own conclusions. What is stated herein is not gospel and there are plenty of other opinions and approaches to consider when selling your home. Readers are encouraged to seek legal and other counsel as appropriate.

Note...

Throughout this book to keep things simple, I refer to a person who is selling real estate as a "real estate agent" or an "agent." There are varying title/role designations for different states. In some states, everyone licensed to sell real estate is referred to as a salesperson and in other states every licensee is referred to as a broker. The reader is encouraged to learn what the real estate licensee designations are in their state and what they mean. The forms that are referenced in this book are specific to Washington State, specifically to the Northwest Multiple Listing Service (NWMLS). These are the most common forms used by NWMLS members to list and sell properties. In some areas of Washington State, other MLS forms (not the NWMLS) are commonly used. Most states in the United States have different MLS systems that are commonly used by real estate agent members. The forms that are referenced in this book are a great jumping off point in terms of the reader learning more about the home selling process. The reader should easily be able to note the forms referenced or the business concept illustrated and find out how that applies in their own real estate market/state.

Okay, that hoop is jumped through, now on to the main event!

TABLE OF CONTENTS

ONE

GETTING ORGANIZED

Selling your home is a pain in the ass. You read correctly, selling your home can be one of the most aggravating and stressful experiences you will go through. The most important thing you can do to help yourself in the home selling process is to first assess your situation and get organized. This book is a great first step for doing just that! Far too many people go about the home selling process with no real plan of action. They just have an agent plant a sign in the yard, hope for the best and call it good. Selling your home is probably the most expensive item you are going to sell and most likely it is your nest egg for retirement or the means to enable you to buy up. It makes good sense for you to get organized and become informed. By doing so, you will remove a lot of the inherent drama and anxiety involved with selling your home and hopefully get top dollar for your property. There are certain advantages and disadvantages when you sell and you need to assess what those are for you and your situation. When you get organized up front and do your homework, you will hopefully make a wiser decision to either sell or not sell.

Your Motivation…

The first question to ask when considering selling your home is, "*What is my motivation?*" Exactly why am I thinking of doing this? Are you considering selling because: everyone says you should, your brother or coworker just sold their home and you want to keep up, all of your neighbors are selling and you think you should too, your parents or children keep nagging you to sell your place, you have to relocate for your job, you have loud and annoying neighbors, you are getting married, you are getting divorced, you are about to have children, you have a child and she needs a bigger home, your children just went off to college or have moved out and you want smaller space, you just got a raise or a promotion, you got an inheritance, you won the lottery, you want a bigger yard, you want more space for a shop or an art studio, you want to live in a different neighborhood, you want to move to a new town, you are retiring and want to downsize, on and on…, whew!

There are many questions to ask and consider. You will catch on real fast that I am a big proponent of answering these questions, getting facts, and becoming informed before you plant a for sale sign in your yard. Do this research and work before you start talking with prospective agents, visiting open houses to see what they look like, or cruising online looking at other places that are for sale. Taking the time to do your homework upfront ensures you will not be bouncing around like a boat without a rudder.

Timeline…

Assuming you answered some of the motivational questions above and you are still thinking about selling your home, the next thing to ponder is your timeline. What kind of mortgage do you currently have? Is it almost paid off or is your property deep in equity loan debt? Are you possibly in a short sale situation (more on that later)? You and the real estate agent you choose to work with will want to review this right off the bat. What is your approximate timeline if you move forward with selling? Where do you plan to live once your place is sold? How are you going to facilitate that transition; i.e. a short term rental after you sell?

It is always good to do a simple review of the pros and cons of selling versus not selling first, before you rush out and list your home for sale. Each situation is unique so you will need to come up with your own checklist of your pros and cons.

Plan B...

You should think ahead as to what your options are if you list your house and it does not sell. Or what if you list your house and it literally sells overnight? Can you be packed up and out of there in 30 or 40 days assuming that is your closing date timeline? Buyers are not as inclined to agree to longer closing time periods anymore and most informed buyers will no longer agree to the old, "*closing plus three*" (more on this later).

So what happens if you list your house in March and it sells right away and you have to be out by the end of April? If you have kids in school, where are you going to live for next two months until their school year ends? Theoretically if a buyer is willing you could have the deal close at the end of April and then have a local real estate attorney write up a lease agreement. Whereby, you rent the house back from the buyer for those two months until your child's school year ends. This would be a standard lease with a security deposit, utility bill arrangements, etc.... However, an educated buyer is most likely not going to want to do this and a smart buyer's agent is never going to advise they agree to this leaseback proposal. If the buyer does agree,

3

then he is now not only the new owner but he is a freshly minted landlord as well. He needs to get insurance to cover a renter, and legally he needs to know what the local landlord/tenant laws are. From his perspective, what if you just flake out and refuse to vacate at the end of your lease (these kinds of stories pop up in the local news around the country every year)? Evicting a tenant is costly and can take a lot of time. No buyer is going to be very keen on doing this, no matter how nice of a seller you may be.

This is where having your "Plan B" in place is important. You need to think through as many possible outcome scenarios as you can before you list your home for sale. Sort of like your junior high math class when you studied those "if, then" math problems. Math really does apply in the real world (Mrs. Ratteree was not kidding back in the eighth grade math class). A good listing agent is going to ask you about this and help you go over and plan for possible outcome scenarios prior to listing your house.

For example, what happens if at the last minute the buyer's loan fails to fund and your deal does not close? If you have already moved out of your property and the day before closing, the buyer's loan does not fund, then they are unable to purchase your house. If they have not waived their financing contingency (via your request on form 22-AR in WA State) they are going to get their earnest money deposit back and you are right back at square one; starting over and putting your house back on the market for sale. You are not going to be pleased, no one is! As a seller, you should be aware of these potential nightmare outcomes ahead of time. They do not happen too frequently but it is best to be aware of them rather than be blindsided by something like this happening with your deal. Being prepared for various outcomes will help if you have moved out and the buyer's loan fails to fund. You will have an idea as to whether or not you are moving back in your home while it is back on the market and waiting for a new buyer or are you going to remain living where you have already moved? If that is the case, what are the financial obligations of doing that? You can and will see, there are many items to ponder prior to listing your house.

Loan Fraud...

Sometimes you can procure a bridge loan and that enables you to list and sell your current house while purchasing your new house. However, this is not always available to many home owners and if not, here is where the issue of loan fraud could arise for you.

A loan officer tells you the only way your deal to purchase will go through is for you to create a "short term" rental agreement. This would be if you are already a current home owner and are purchasing a new house and you intend to sell your current house after your new house deal closes. The loan person encourages you to have a friend or family member with a different last name fill out the bogus rental agreement and have you collect a fake rental security deposit. This is usually presented as if there is nothing to it, just business as usual, no big deal. Once your deal closes you of course won't be renting your current property and no one will be the wiser. This is completely illegal! If you agree to participate, i.e. procure a fake lease, then you are directly involved in committing loan fraud. Don't go there! Of course, this kind of scenario is typically presented to the borrower right before they are set to close on their new property, while they still own their current home, so they are in an extremely stressful situation. If their loan officer cannot deliver their loan as promised, then most likely the buyer loses the house they are purchasing and possibly their earnest money deposit. If they agree to the bogus rent-back scheme their lender has proposed then they are committing a crime. Not a nice situation! In this case, it is best to immediately consult with a real estate attorney and report this to the appropriate state board or committee that oversees the financial institution industry in your state.

Self Torture...

Are you thinking about selling your house yourself, not using an agent or paying a flat fee for a limited service brokerage? The header above is somewhat cheeky but true! Why not sell your own house? All you have to do is buy a sign, stick it in the yard, take some pictures, make some flyers, put the word out that your castle is for sale and away you go! I suppose that could be true. There are properties that the owner does sell by himself, without an agent's help. However, I have not heard very many for sale by owner success stories.

If you are not going to sell completely solo, maybe you think you will pay a flat fee and have a limited service brokerage list your property for you. This type of service sometimes provides you with basic seller disclosure forms, puts a sign in your yard, and lists your property in the local MLS (multiple listing service). That's it. They state in the listing posted online that all buyer agents must work directly with the seller, do not contact the limited service brokerage with any questions or offers. As a strong buyer's agent I can tell you this does not thrill buyers or their agent. First, my experience with these types of listings is the seller is completely clueless about what to do, the protocols of an offer, the whole process. They usually start to ask me, the buyer's agent, questions that a listing agent needs to be there to answer and help them with. Legally I am representing my buyer; I cannot answer a limited service brokerage/for sale by owner, seller question. Any buyer's agent that does so is entering into a legal abyss and should know better. More than once, I have referred sellers who are using these limited service brokerages or representing themselves to a local real estate attorney for help. I have never yet had a buyer that has actually completed a purchase with a limited brokerage service seller or a for sale by owner property. That doesn't mean these sales do not happen but I haven't had any of these deals work out and I do not hear many success stories out there from other agents regarding this type of sale.

I am partial to the full service agent model as that is how I have always worked. If I thought another way of doing business would serve my clients better and enable me to make a better living, I would be doing it. A full service agent is an agent that educates and works with you the seller from the start of the listing process all the way through to the end and then follows up with you and perhaps helps you buy another property when yours has sold. This person is your guide through the whole selling process, your go-to person and the person who is in charge of managing all aspects of your property's listing, deal negotiation and getting your deal closed.

Here is why I think selling without a full service listing agent helping you might not be the best idea.

1.   Do you know a good local real estate attorney that you trust who can help you with every step involved when it comes to reviewing an offer you may get? Do you have an attorney who can ensure you are using legal purchase and sale forms? Is there someone on your side who will make sure you are following all the legal timelines and providing the buyer with the right forms as required by law?

2.   Do you know a good title company you can hire to order your preliminary title report and to handle title once you have a deal?

3.   Do you know how to get a copy of the required forms you may need to provide a buyer with? Depending on the age of your house and your state's real estate laws this could include: a Lead Disclosure form, the Seller Disclosure Statement, the Legal Description, etc....

4.   Are you prepared to handle negotiations directly with a buyer's agent? Presumably, the buyer's agent knows their way around the purchase and sale agreement forms, all of the deadlines and loopholes and will be advocating on their client's behalf; i.e. not answering your questions about the forms presented or letting you know what steps you as a seller need to take, etc....

5. Are you prepared to handle endless phone calls from prospective buyer's agents and the general public asking you questions about your home, asking to see it?

6. Are you prepared to be available for each showing, assuming you do not put a key box up for agent access?

7. Are you aware of what safety precautions you need to take when staying at home and letting a prospective buyer tour your house or vacating your home and letting a buyer and their agent tour?

8. Do you know the best way to follow up and contact agents or the public who have seen your home for feedback? Do you know the right questions to ask when soliciting feedback?

9. Can your ego take the sometimes unflattering feedback you may get? Will you be able to best tell what feedback is useful and what to ignore?

10. You may ask, *"If I sell by myself or use a limited service broker, then won't I save a lot of money?"* Perhaps, but that is statistically doubtful. It is true, selling your home is not inexpensive and in real estate you get what you pay for. There are successful agents who specialize in tracking and converting for sale by owner properties. How it that possible? Because they know that statistically most for sale by owner properties do not sell. The time your property will sit on the market as a for sale by owner property is statistically longer, with less showings, and exposure. How

much money does that ultimately cost you? If you are doing this solo, then the expense for the real estate attorney who needs to review everything is not going to be insignificant and what is your time worth?

11. What about the intangible costs, the stress and uncertainty of trying to sell something you are so attached to in a profession/work arena you are not well versed in?

I have been licensed in the residential real estate industry since 1991 and whenever I have bought or sold my own home I always hire another full service real estate agent to help me. Why would I do that? I already know the forms, requirements, protocols backwards and forwards. I always hire an agent to represent me, because I know I am going to get stressed out, lose my mind when selling (and buying) and I know firsthand the value of having a good agent there every step of the way to help me focus and calm down. They are the neutral third party that can keep things moving along. Every seller's ego is tied up in their house. I don't care how Zen master you have become, you have some attachment to your nest and it almost impossible to be detached about your home; there are far too many issues, memories and emotions involved.

Every seller thinks their castle is the bomb and knows all the reasons why their home is worth more than the show pony home that is listed for sale down the street; just like all parents think their children are special or gifted. In my opinion, all sellers can greatly benefit from having an objective, full service real estate agent represent them. At a minimum, a good listing agent can help the seller's ego accept the reality of the current market and the conditions and limitations of their home. Does any of this ring true, make sense? If not, go ahead and list your home for sale by yourself or with a do-it-yourself, limited brokerage service. If you succeed and manage to get it all done and done legally, kudos! However, know that most for sale by owner properties languish on the market and by the time the owner comes to reason and hires an agent to represent him, the prime exposure window has been wasted, not to mention the stress. And as they say, "*time is money.*"

Real Life…

It is often tempting to think about just listing your home for sale yourself, that is until the reality of doing so hits (the endless phone calls, pushy agents, complex legal forms, negotiation, etc…). Short of trying to sell their house completely solo, some home owners are tempted to use a limited service brokerage. These are brokerages that usually will plant a for sale sign in your yard, officially list your property in the local multiple listing service (MLS) and that is it. You are on your own with any offers and all the important details like title, escrow, closing. When I represent buyers, sometimes we will come across one of these limited service brokerage listings. I always warn my buyers in advance that in my experience, it usually is not an easy ride. The seller is typically fairly clueless as to what has to happen with an offer and legally I am not allowed to answer and help the seller out.

A few years ago, I had some buyers and we saw several listings and one of them was a limited service brokerage listing. According to the active and sold comp data I pulled for my buyers, this house was

11

priced below the actual market price and for no apparent reason, except lack of knowledge on the seller's part is my guess. My buyers decided they wanted to make an offer on this house. I called the seller direct, as the listing report stated all agents were to contact and work directly with the seller. I let the seller know I had pre-approved buyers who were interested in making an offer. First, the buyers would like to see the seller disclosure statement (Form 17 in WA State) and we would need a copy of the legal description as well (a mutually acknowledged legal description is required in WA State in order for an offer to be considered mutually accepted). The seller had no idea what I was talking about. I asked if their title company had provided them with a copy of the legal description when they issued a preliminary title report upon listing. That question got me dead air. The seller had no clue as to what was legally and organizationally necessary to review an offer. He began asking me about these items and I had to politely let him know that I represent the buyers, I cannot legally answer his questions, help out and advise with things on his end. I suggested he contact his limited service brokerage to see if they could help and/or a local real estate attorney.

In the meantime, I let my buyers know the seller was clueless as to the offer process but they decided to go ahead and make an offer and see what happened. So the next day, we wrote up their offer and I called the seller back and asked how I should submit my buyer's offer (in person, by fax, by email)? The seller was again completely out of touch and began asking me the same questions as the day before. I told him that legally I needed to present my buyer's offer and it expired the next day at 9 p.m. I drove to his house and handed off the offer to him. He again tried to get me to advise him as to how to review the offer, what certain forms were, etc.... He then told me he had gotten another offer yesterday. This is something he should have told me prior to my buyers writing up their offer. He began to tell me some of the terms of the other offer (something he should not have done). From what I could tell, the other offer was from buyers who did not yet have a loan pre-approval and it did not sound like they even had an earnest money deposit. I again advised he hire a local real estate attorney to help him since his limited service listing brokerage was not helping (and nor should they as their listing contract plainly states they do not assist with offers period). I let my buyers know what had happened when I delivered their offer and about the competing offer. The following evening I called the seller, as I had not heard anything back and my buyers' offer was set to expire in an hour. He proudly told me he had accepted the other offer yesterday afternoon. Thanks for the courtesy notice! He then persisted in asking me questions about the other offer he had accepted, I politely refused to comment and hung up.

My buyers were not that disappointed as they knew from the start how this situation could go and true to form it went that way; i.e. a seller trying to run the show who had no clue what he was doing. We found a better house and they made an offer and it was accepted. About two weeks later, this limited service brokerage seller called me up and said he had decided to accept my buyers' offer. What? I let him know my buyers' offer had expired over two weeks ago and in addition he had already accepted another offer for his property. He then went into a long rant as to how the other offer was bogus and those buyers couldn't afford his house (big surprise they were not even pre-approved for a loan) and how his limited service brokerage had offered no help, etc.... He could not quite understand that my buyers had moved on and that their offer had expired. He kept trying to insist that my buyers were obligated to purchase his house now. I gave him the names of some local real estate attorneys and suggested he contact them for help.

Had this seller had even the most basic of help in listing his home for sale, he could have had a multiple offer scenario for his property, perhaps bid up the sale price. He certainly would have had qualified buyers making bids; i.e. any good listing agent is going to inform a buyer's agent that the seller prefers to only see offers from verified buyers who are pre-approved for a home loan. They will ask for a copy of that pre-approval and check-in with the loan person who issued it. This story shows you why I think it is in a seller's best interest to hire a full time, full service agent and brokerage to represent them in the sale of their home. It also illustrates why becoming informed before you list your house for sale is crucial! Please do not rush out and sign on with the brokerage that is the cheapest without doing your homework. It is in your bank account's best interest to take your time up front and do your research and fully understand what it is you are doing.

TWO

CHOOSING YOUR AGENT

Assuming you made it through chapter one, you have weighed the pros and cons of selling that are specific to your situation and you have decided to proceed with selling your property. The next step is to find the best full service agent to represent you.

Finding an Agent...

Do you plan on hiring the agent who originally sold you the house? Is she still in business, did you like her, has she stayed in touch with you in the years since you purchased, can she do a good job working as your listing agent? If those answers are yes, then you should put her on your list to interview. Even if you are 99% sure you will use your former agent to list your house, you should still interview a few more real estate agents so you have an informed overview of what kind of representation is currently available and who is the best fit for you.

How do you find a full service real estate agent to work with? Naturally you can search online, jot down agent names that are plastered on the bus stop benches and grocery carts, ask friends and family who they worked with, talk to your second cousin Bill who just got his real estate license, call the agent who just listed the house for sale down the street, etc.... I would first like to remind you that this is likely the most expensive item you will sell in your lifetime or it will rank right up there. It is not like you are having a yard sale and getting rid of a few used items you no longer need. You dump your used brick-brack on a table in the front lawn and any price a potential buyer might offer you is okay by you, so long as they haul it all away before the end of the day. Selling your home is not like a yard sale, throw it all out on the lawn and see what happens! This is why doing your research and getting organized ahead of time is crucial.

No Friends or Family...

I personally do not work with someone I am related to or am close friends with. Here's why. Let's say you are an agent and your sister is going to sell her house. Simple, she will list with you and you will be her agent right? No! There might be all sorts of unresolved sibling rivalry issues still at play. Subconsciously you might not want your sister selling her current place and getting something better than what you have. You most likely will make assumptions or suggestions that you should not, "*I know my sister won't mind if I suggest we remove the living room furniture that I have always thought was tacky.*" A suggestion to remove items in order to enhance the listing are usually better received when a neutral, third party makes it. If you are your sister's agent there is too much history and family baggage to clutter your thinking and old battles can quickly resurface. You won't be as objective or neutral, as an unrelated listing agent will be. Also, what if you are your sister's agent and you make a huge mistake or screw something up with her deal? Say she misses out on a great offer and rightly or wrongly she holds you (her agent) responsible. Thanksgivings spent together are going to be real fun with her sitting there resenting you for making her miss out on a great offer. It may not even be true that you the agent did anything to hamper her deal and cause her to miss out but the perception of that is still there. In my opinion, having a family member act as your listing agent and selling your house usually do not mix well together.

Next, there is your best friend Sheila who is a long time licensed real estate agent. She is all gung-ho to help you sell your place. I always caution that the same problems with a family member might happen with a friend. Also, your friend working as your real estate agent might not be on her toes as much as she would be with a neutral client. There is a good chance that agent Sheila will be a bit more lax, *"Oh, I'm 40 minutes late but Chris won't mind because we are friends and he knows I'm always running late."* Or, *"Legally I need Chris to fill this form out tonight but we are friends and I know he won't sue me so we'll just do it later."* The professional boundaries get blurred; the agent is not as alert. If you become annoyed with the job your friend (agent Sheila) is doing and you want to switch to another listing agent, how awkward is that going to be? It could put a real damper on your friendship. So why bother, don't go there.

Contrary to what you may think or have heard, pick someone who is professional, has a good track record, with whom you click, but who is not related to you or a good friend. It keeps things simple. There is enough inherent drama and emotion involved in selling a house; you don't need to add family and friendship baggage to the mix! If you are pressured by others to use family or a friend to represent you, tell them it is nothing personal, just business. You like to keep your business affairs separate from your personal life. If their egos can't handle that response, then that is their problem to work out.

There is too much money involved in selling a house for this process not to be a business venture and treated accordingly.

Another point to make on this topic of family and friends is if they represent you, then they are going to know all of your business, literally. They will know what you can and cannot afford to sell your place for. If you are selling with a spouse or partner, they will see up close and personal how you two interact. Suddenly your world of friends and family knows all of your personal business. *"She can't afford to sell her house for less than X amount. He's a rude jerk when he reviews offers. She really is a picky princess. They are indecisive. They fight like cats and dogs, is their marriage on the rocks?"* Even if you work with a friend or family member who does not gossip, sometimes things slip out by accident. If you choose to work with someone who is outside of your family and friend sphere, a neutral and competent professional, then your personal business should stay where it belongs, in the vault! If you pick a person who is outside of your sphere who is an enormous gossip (and legally they shouldn't be gabbing about you), who are they going to gossip with, their dog? They don't know your friends and family and so your personal information remains private.

The Referral...

Then there is the referral. Let's say your sister or coworker has a real estate agent that they think is absolutely wonderful. That is good to know, take it into consideration. However, do not go on autopilot and think, *"My search is over, I'll just work with Bob because Suzie says Bob is the best."* Suzie may very well be correct and agent Bob is the best. But you still should do your own vetting and make sure you agree with

Suzie's strong recommendation. You might be surprised to learn that Suzie gets a referral fee (legal in some states and illegal in others) from this awesome agent named Bob for referring you to him. You may discover Suzie is naive and this agent is a terrific manipulator, well versed in stroking egos (more about manipulators later). Just make sure you personally investigate those who are referred to you and that they meet the criteria of what you are looking for. Do not assume that since X referred this agent to me then they must be fine and that's all I need to know or do. Doing that would be working on autopilot on your part and it can (and usually does) come back to bite you.

No Newbie's, Retirees, Dilettantes, Part-timers...

I would personally avoid a new real estate agent. Clearly, everyone has to start somewhere and get established but it would be far better for you to have an experienced agent, who has been around the race track and in the trenches a few hundred times or more. A newbie might be nice, diligent, and ethical but their lack of hands-on experience can backfire. There are ways for a newbie to build their career. They could start out as a licensed agent's assistant or they could pair up for a year or so with a seasoned broker or mentor who is hands-on involved with each step of their transactions to ensure things are not overlooked. Meaning, the new agent trails the experienced agent and acts essentially as their gopher, learns the business side by side. Beware the new agent who says all is good because his managing broker or the designated broker will be personally reviewing all his paperwork. They do that for all agents regardless of their experience level and years in the business. In my opinion, the hands-on help is

19

needed out in the field and when listing your place and helping you negotiate when you receive an offer, not after the fact. A newbie in this field who say previously sold cars or skin care products, or recently earned their MBA is not really up to speed in my opinion. This does not mean the newbie is not well intentioned or intelligent. They just do not have (in my opinion) the practical, hands-on and intuitive experience that is necessary and crucial to ensure your home selling experience is as easy as it can be.

The real estate industry has a history of taking on anyone who has done the cursory training for a license. Unfortunately, the industry joke has long been, *"If you can breathe on a mirror and you like people then you are in business. Go out there and fly by the seat of your pants, fake it until you make it or fail."* Most do not succeed big surprise. This is part of the reason why real estate is such a high turnover industry. And the in-house training that brokerages used to require for new agents continues to diminish as this industry changes. Not that a majority of that kind of education was ever very helpful. I personally found it to be little more than a glorified charm school; i.e. learn to dress for success, corporate rah-rah, and manipulation skills 101.

Next, there is the retired grandma and dilettante real estate agent. These are typically well meaning individuals who are retired and/or independently wealthy. They are looking for a little diversion or an identity to make their life a bit more interesting, so they decide to sell real estate. In my experience, these can be some of the worst agents out there. They are not really motivated to stay on top of the constantly changing rules, forms, and laws that this industry is known for. These agents tend to putter about and make a sale in between their holiday trips, their social club events, and their winters in Palm Springs. They are pretty much playing real estate agent to keep themselves occupied. I would advise finding an agent who is working this business full time, who is out there making deals, committed first to their work, not their leisure life. That said, you do not have to hire a Type A nut bucket either, a balance is nice. A super busy agent will not have as much time to spend with you. As a side note, just because someone is a senior citizen and looks like Mr. or Mrs. Santa Claus, does not mean that they are ethical or competent. Please do not go on autopilot because someone's looks conjures up warm and fuzzy, childhood story book images for you or they are so model perfect and sexy that you overlook the fact that they are dumber than a post. Hang out with Mr. and Mrs. Claus at bingo night or stop by Hooters or Chippendale's if you want to ogle flesh.

Finally, there are the part-timer agents, my least favorite. These people have full time jobs/careers and think they can make big bucks on the side by selling real estate for all their family, friends, and co-workers. Contrary to what many may say or believe, real estate is not a part time job. To do this job effectively and provide a seller with the best level of service, I think your agent needs to be a full time, full service agent. I cringe whenever I call a listing agent, only to be connected to their voice mail at their full time job at one of the local corporations or governmental agencies; don't these big entities have anti moonlighting clauses in their employee contracts? When something crucial regarding the transaction is needed in the middle of the workday, where are these charming part time agents? In a staff meeting at their real job! In my experience, these folks rarely are on top of real estate laws, inventory, or the correct way of doing business. How could they be? They already have a full time job. A part-timer does not have the time to preview listings and know firsthand the current state of the market, what your house should be listed for. Online previewing while at work at their full time job, does not give an agent a true understanding of the inventory or the current state of the market. Nor is Ms. Part-timer who is trying to postpone a buyer's offer to suit her full time work schedule's time constraints very consumer friendly either.

Usually the full time, full service agent involved in a deal with a part time agent has to essentially take over the deal and work both ends of it to make it come together and happen. The part time agent still ends up with their portion of the commission even though you have paid this person to do work they have pushed off onto the buyer's agent. You the seller will not typically have a clue this has happened, as the buyer's agent cannot legally give you a call and let you know he is doing all the work on this deal and your part time agent is not doing squat to earn the commission you are paying her. I have observed these part time agents eventually lose their license for incompetence or negligence or their clients begin to figure out part time means less for them and quit using them. These agents typically go out of business. Or they pick up the clue phone and start working this job full time and providing the level of full time service that their clients deserve and the legalities of this business demands.

I think there is one possible exception for a part time agent. If the agent lives in a rural location, say a remote town of 5,000 residents or less, or they are on a small vacation island, then unless they are independently wealthy they probably will need to have another full time job in order to survive. Real estate is truly part time where they live as there is not much inventory to cover, not many transactions happening, and way less to keep up on. In my opinion, any agent who is good and working in a metro area should be able to sell real estate full time and offer full service to their clients. Again, selling your home is probably the most expensive thing you will sell, why have a part-timer represent you?

The Big Lister...

This is the agent who has listings oozing out of their pores. They usually will try and dazzle you with the volume of listings they have and make you believe they must be in the know and good because they have so many listings. That could be true but you still should do your due diligence. Another point to consider, even if they are a great agent, if they are representing a ton of active listings, then they are not going to have a lot of time to spend with you and your listing; they already have loads of other sellers and properties they are already dealing with. Unfortunately, many big listing agents are also known in the industry as those who "buy listings." These are types who list a property at any price point, who cares how over priced it is because for them it is all about getting their sign in another front yard and having another active listing to tout so everyone thinks they are a great agent. Some agents with many listings truly are great agents and unfortunately

23

many are not. You will see as you read on the various criteria I suggest
you look for and signs to watch out for and that will help you decide
what to focus on. I would advise taking the number of listings an
agent currently has or has had with a grain of salt. It is certainly, I do
not think the ultimate deciding factor in choosing the best agent to
represent you and your property.

Interviewing Agents…

When you have your short list of real estate agents to interview,
try to get a sense when you meet with a prospective agent of how he
works. Is their personality a good match for yours? Do they know
what they are doing or are they all charm and no substance? What is
their seller information packet like? Is it informative and educational
or just pre-made corporate bunk their company provides with glossy
stock image photos and not much substance? Do they have a pre-
made iPad or laptop company video and try and wow you with bells
and whistles? Have they gone completely Hollywood and instead of
meeting with you, they email you a video about themselves and their
company? Technology can be useful but in this game, hands-on
information that actually educates and true competence is crucial. It is
great if your real estate agent has a good personality and you enjoy their
company. However, the most important part is if they are informative,
competent, ethical, timely and organized. When it comes down to the
purchase and sale forms, the offer timelines, negotiation, can they
deliver? A **tip**, just because an agent is a "top producer" or well
known, does not automatically mean they are ethical or good, especially
from a consumer standpoint.

24

Questions to Ask an Agent...

Here is a list of questions you may want to ask a real estate agent when you interview them to list your house. After the list is more detailed information on each question's topic. I hope this list helps fire up your brain. You may have questions of your own to add based on your specific situation and needs.

1. How many years have you been working as an active and licensed real estate agent?

2. What do these titles, designations, abbreviations, listed on your business card mean?

3. Are you a member of NAR?

4. Do you do dual agency?

5. Are you a full time, full service agent? Will I be working directly with you from the start of my search until the end?

6. Will you offer me a discount, refund or credit if I list with you?

7. Where are the active and sold comp sheets?

8. Do you tour comparable properties?

9. What if I do not agree with the suggested list price?

10. Where is my estimated seller's net proceeds sheet?

11. What are some typical out-of-pocket expenses that I need to know about for the home selling process?

12. How many clients are you currently working with and what is your client limit?

13. Did you write the information contained in your seller packet?

14. What sort of references can you provide?

15. Do you specialize in a particular neighborhood or area?

16. Have you ever been sued by a former client or disciplined by any real estate professional organization? (i.e. the local MLS, board of Realtors, state licensing board)

17. Have you ever been convicted of a crime or been incarcerated?

18. What is your level of education?

Question One: You want to know how long they have been selling real estate. Did they just get their license? Do they sell real estate full time? How long have they sold real estate in your state? Are they up on the laws/business norms in your state?

Question Two: Ask them to explain what their title or designations on their business card mean. Some titles and designations are less impressive than you might imagine (bordering on made up). I won't pick on any specific ones here but use your common sense. You can also research these titles online as well. If you read the "Note" at the start of this book, you know I am generically referring to anyone who is licensed to sell real estate as either an agent or real estate agent. Different states have different terms. In Washington State, everyone who has a real estate license is now referred to as a Broker. Then there is a Managing Broker level, which in Washington State means they have had an active real estate licensee for three years worked full time as an agent for those years, have additional training, passed more tests, and they can legally open and operate their own real estate brokerage and/or manage other brokers in the office. Finally there is the Designated Broker who is the person appointed to run the real estate office, through whom disputes are ultimately mediated. There is the Owner (sometimes they also act as the Designated Broker) and they own the brokerage. You may want to find out what the titles are and how they work in your state. As you can see, being called a real estate Broker in Washington State is not something to be impressed with. It just means the person has a basic license to sell real estate.

Question Three: NAR is the National Association of Realtors. What do you the consumer care about this? Well, if an agent pays annual dues and is a member of NAR, then there is another level of protection should things go wrong. If you have serious problems with your agent and she is a Realtor, then you can report her to NAR and file a complaint against her behavior with them. The regional branch of NAR will most likely intervene and look into to your grievances. Conceivably, if your agent is really bad, then NAR might kick her out for her unethical behavior. So there is some extra assurance if your agent is a member of NAR (a Realtor) that they must uphold the NAR Code of Ethics and be more accountable. You can Google this topic and visit the NAR website if you want to learn more.

To add a bit of confusion to this, there is the term Realtor. That is a trademarked word, coined and owned by the National Association of Realtors. Pronounced "real" and "tor" there is no "i" in the spelling or correct pronunciation; i.e. "*Realitor*" or "*Realiter*" is

27

incorrect. Those who are not dues paying members of NAR are not permitted to use the word Realtor or the Realtor logo.

Question Four: I hope they answer no! Dual agency is not legal in some states but currently it is legal in Washington State. Dual agency means your real estate agent is representing you the seller and the buyer in the transaction. They are going to keep their mouth shut and neutrally represent both parties and incidentally they are going to collect a double commission for working both sides of the transaction. I have never understood ethically how this works. In my opinion, no one can remain neutral when they are representing both sides of a deal. At a minimum there is body language, word slips, tone of voice, etc.... For me, dual agency has always been analogous to an attorney representing both the plaintiff and the defendant. How would that work to either party's advantage except the agent's bank account? I have never done a dual agency deal because I do not think they are fair to either the seller or the buyer. Quite a few agents, some very successful, do act as a dual agents. I would suggest you the client not agree to that. The purchase and sale agreement (in Washington State) has boxes where the agent indicates who they are representing.

Here is a **tip** about dual agency. When you drive around and see big time agent X's for sale signs, note when you see one of his yard signs and on top of it is a "sold" sign rider with his name on it too. Most likely, this agent is proudly letting you know that he represented both the seller and buyer in this sale. You can see via the signs that some agents tout this as a great thing; great for whom?

In my case, since I do not do dual agency, if I take a listing (let's say it is a two bedroom townhouse in the south end listed for $285,000) and one of my buyers is looking at properties that this listing's criteria falls under (i.e. two bedroom townhouse in the south end priced $300,000 and below). I immediately notify my buyer that I have taken this listing. If they have interest in seeing it, I refer them to another real estate agent to work with for this specific listing only. If they tour my seller's listing and decide to make an offer, then the other agent represents them. If they do not have an interest in my listing, then we continue to work together and look at other listings that are not mine. This keeps things real simple, fair, and it's not difficult to work this way.

One point to note, your listing agent may refer one of her buyer clients to another agent who works in her brokerage. For example, your agent hangs her license with XYZ Realty that is her brokerage. She does not do dual agency so she refers her buyer client who is interested in your house to Amy who also hangs her license with XYZ Realty, the same brokerage. Technically, XYZ Realty is the brokerage for both of these agents. If one of their agents represents the buyer in the sale of one of their other agent's listings, one could also call this dual agency. My point for you is that the same agent does not represent both the buyer and the seller in a single transaction. As long as there are two different agents, one representing the seller and one representing the buyer in a transaction, I do not see a conflict of interest or a problem with both of the agents having their licenses hanging in the same brokerage, XYZ Realty. The agents are not (should not be) colluding behind the scenes regardless if they are from the same brokerage or two completely different brokerages.

Question Five: We touched on the full service agent topic a few pages back. This is the traditional, one person going through the entire deal with you, helping you, being accountable, etc.... I am partial to this method because I think the seller is better served not being passed off to different people in various stages of their deal.

Question Six: If you are selling your home and purchasing another house using a new mortgage to accomplish this, then the refund or credit your listing agent may offer to give you at closing or after closing can trigger issues with the loan end of things for your new purchase. Any money that is coming back to you, being paid to you either before a deal closes or after, needs to be reported to the lender who is putting together your new mortgage for your new house. They legally have to take into account this refunded money as it could potentially screw up your loan/income ratio. If you do not report money that is being refunded or paid to you (either at closing or afterwards), then you most likely are committing loan fraud which typically falls in the felony category. Obviously, if your new home purchase is all cash (no financing) then this does not apply. However, anyone that has to pay (credit/refund) or discount their commission in order to entice a seller to list with them is a red flag in my opinion. Why do they have to pay clients to list with them, are they desperate, incompetent? Does your accountant, lawyer, dentist, pay you to work with them?

Question Seven: A good listing agent is going to provide you with two statistical sheets which show active and sold listings. The active comps (comparisons) will list all houses in your home's immediate radius that are the same size; i.e. other three bedroom, two bath homes that are currently listed for sale. This will provide you with an average list price and show you how many days these properties have been on the market. The sold comp sheet will be for properties like yours in your home's immediate radius that have sold in say the last three months, farther back if there have been no recent sales. It will show you the list price, the average sale price and the days they sat on the market before they sold. Your agent should also note on these sheets which properties are short sales or foreclosure properties as they do not directly equate to your listing if you are not in that situation. These sheets should be provided to you when you are at the point where you are determining what your list price will be and updated for you again when you receive and review an offer.

Question Eight: Does this agent offer to take you on a tour of comparable properties before you decide on your list price? A good listing agent wants to not only tell you about the comparable listings, via the sheets I mentioned above, but they also want to show you what comparable properties in your area actually look like. When possible, this agent should set up a tour for you and you all should go out and physically see the houses on the market that will be your closest competition. This way you get a firsthand overview of the market,

what you are up against and you will be able to see things from a
buyer's perspective; i.e. what will they most likely be looking at besides
your wonderful house? You can discover ideas for making your home
look more appealing and you will note any factors that cannot be
changed with your property that another listing has and works in its
favor. For example, the house three blocks over that is the nearest
competitive listing to yours has a large family room and a pool. Your
house does not have those features, so you know from the start what
you are up against. Or you know that whoever buys your house is not
going to be interested in a large family room or a swimming pool. A
good listing agent will arrange to take you out to see these properties
before you determine your list price. Not all properties that are nearby
are going to be easily accessible, some require special appointments for
showings, etc... and it's not fair to waste that seller's time as you are
not interested in purchasing their property. But there should be
enough vacant or easily accessible properties for sale nearby to tour so
that you can get a good idea of what it out there.

Question Nine: At some point, hopefully after you have been educated
via active and sold comps and a tour, a prospective agent is going to
provide you with a suggested list price or perhaps a suggested range for
your list price. Ask the agent if they will still list your house if you want
the list price to be significantly more than their suggested list
price/range. If they say yes, I would pass on working with them. Any
agent who lists a property that they know is overpriced based on the
active/sold comps and the current state of the market, is doing what is

commonly referred to in this business as "*buying a listing.*" These types of agents know you will not get the high price you think your property is worth and they are banking on wearing you down as your home languishes on the market until you come to reason a month or so later and agree to reduce the list price to the range they originally suggested. Nothing is worse for your property. The longer your house sits on the market, the more concern a prospective buyer may have, "*What is wrong with this place? Why hasn't it sold yet?*" Also, if it is overpriced you have missed out on buyers who could afford your house if it were priced right. For example, the comps and current market show your house's list price should be $350,000. You insist it is worth $400,000 and you get a listing agent who agrees to list it for that price if you agree to reduce the list price if it hasn't sold in a few weeks, or a month. During the time your house sits overpriced at $400,000 you miss out on a buyer who is looking in your area and is pre-approved to purchase up to $350,000. They buy something else when they could have purchased your home. You do not get any offers at your high list price and a couple of months later your listing agent has now got you down to a list price of $350,000 or less. The house then finally sells after it has sat on the market. Usually if a house is overpriced and sits and then months later the price is reduced, a buyer is psychologically going to wonder what is wrong with the place, why it was overpriced? They are more inclined to offer less for your house because of the time it has sat on the market. That might seem illogical. If the house is now finally priced correctly weeks or months later, why would a buyer still offer less? When I am a buyer's agent I see this quite a bit. Often even when I try and explain to the buyer that the house was not priced correctly to begin with but it is now priced accurately, they still think they should offer less because it has been listed for a while. As a seller, I would suggest pricing your house right from day one and only hire a listing agent who will list your house if it is priced correctly from the start. I do not think you want someone to list your house with an agent who is then going to try and wear you down over time on the list price. There are many successful listing agents who work this way and it's your choice if you want to go that route or not.

Question Ten: When you are deciding what your list price is going to be your agent should provide you with an estimated seller's net proceeds sheet which outlines various fees and what your outlay and hopefully gain will be if the house sells at list price. The agent should include some other sale price points as well for reference and of course include the absolute rock bottom sale price, whereby you are just breaking even, covering all the costs in order to sell your home. You should review this information prior to signing a listing agreement. A good listing agent will have you initial this sheet as proof that you reviewed it prior to listing.

Question Eleven: Some typical out of pocket expenses that you need to plan for when selling include money to fix up and prepare your house for listing, money set aside for repair items that may come up during a buyer's inspection which they request you fix before the deal closes. Then there are the other funds you need to close the deal; i.e. paying off your existing mortgage, home equity line of credit, any back taxes or home owner dues and any special assessments. Yes, you are going to need some actual cash on hand in order to sell your home.

Question Twelve: You want to ask about their current client load to make sure your agent is not on her way to overload. Real estate is a high burnout industry. Your agent needs to have boundaries and know when she is reaching her limit. Listings take time and a good seller's agent is going to make sure she has the necessary time to devote to you. Some agents might be able to work effectively with eight sellers at one time, others three sellers. There is no magic answer. It is just important that your agent has thought about this and knows their personal burnout limit and knows how to pace themselves accordingly.

Question Thirteen: The information in the real estate agent's seller packet should be educational, informative, and hopefully something they have personally written and customized. The worst case is you do not even get a seller packet. Or you get one that is four-color, corporate-neutered fluff that looks nice and is provided by the brokerage to the agent and usually it is not very informative. Hopefully the seller packet information outlines the home selling process for you, includes a sample purchase and sale agreement to review and has other required legal disclosure forms such as the Federal Government's Lead Disclosure booklet. In Washington State you are also required to receive the Law of Agency booklet prior to listing. I think it is best you receive all of this information, legally required or not, up front before you list your home for sale. This way you have time to read it and ask questions before you are excited about and distracted by an offer.

Question Fourteen: Are the former client testimonials your agent provides legit? Is there a full name by the glowing rave, not just "J. Smith?" Or worse, a glowing blurb with no name or initials next to it, gee I wonder who wrote that? Just because a nice comment about the agent is supposed to be from a legitimate client does not make it so. This is the same with online reviews. Just because an agent, product, service is highly ranked online does not necessarily mean it is legitimate. There are now companies that agents can hire to do nothing but go online and write rave reviews about the agent. And yes, there are agents who troll the internet and post fake, negative comments about their competitors. So be discerning. Does the agent you are interviewing have former clients and industry professionals (such as escrow, real estate attorneys, and inspectors) that you can contact directly for a reference if you choose?

Question Fifteen: There are many agents who choose to specialize in a certain area or neighborhood. This would be the specialist agent of Jackal Heights. You know the agent who has her face plastered on every shopping cart in the neighborhood and joins every community committee, and stops at almost nothing so she can plant her for sale yard signs in as many lots in Jackal Heights as possible.

Back in the old days, (meaning the early 1990s) this kind of neighborhood specialist was more common and it was more of a benefit for the seller. Agents were much more area specific or neighborhood specialists back then, because many states did not have electronic key boxes. Keys for listed properties were still picked up and returned to the neighborhood listing office. Listings were not posted online like today. Back then hard copy, black and white listing books were published and delivered to the brokerages once a week. Agents used to literally fight over the office copies of the listing books. That is where an agent found out about new listings, got the latest property status information. It seems hard to believe. When I first started in the business, this was still the common practice; the internet was very new in the real estate industry. Pocket listings and secret deals were much more common. An agent typically picked a neighborhood or small geographic area and specialized in it. Thankfully, the internet changed all of this. Now agents have full access to all member listings posted online at their local MLS, and the public has some access as well. This put a big damper on pocket listings and insider neighborhood deals. Now most listings have key boxes for access so the agent no longer has to go by the local listing brokerage's office when touring or previewing to pick up keys. Thus, a competent seller's agent can now effectively cover a much wider geographic area.

Question Sixteen: If they were taken to court by a former client, what was the outcome, were they cleared of the charges? Has the MLS disciplined or fined them for breaking rules, any complaints at the department of licensing against them? You can ask these questions directly and someone who is honest and secure will not be offended by such questions. If you ask and they act annoyed, shocked, dismayed, then why is that? Given the reputation that some in this industry have, I think these questions are legitimate and easily answered without attitude if they are on the up and up. Don't feel embarrassed to ask these questions even if the agent is Mr. Luxury Real Estate and has 400 sales a year. You can also search online to see if they have been sued or if there are any news articles concerning something they were involved in that is not above board. It amazes me, the number of people who innocently choose to work with crooks, or former crooks. With a simple internet search and a bit of probing you can have answers to these kinds of questions.

Question Seventeen: In some states a convicted felon or someone who served time in the big house for fraud, embezzlement, assault, walks out of jail and gets their real estate license. Some states now require felony background checks and fingerprint new agents but not all. So be alert and do your homework! There are various online investigative services you can use to look up and investigate anyone from your nanny to your agent and loan person. Some states offer such a service via their state highway patrol website. For a nominal fee, you can look up a person and learn if they have been in trouble with the law or not.

Question Eighteen: There are no strict educational requirements for a real estate licensee outside of the cursory class training hours, exam, and in some states there is a high school diploma or GED requirement. I have worked with agents who barely graduated junior high and others who have PhDs and both were competent. However, I would want to ask about an agent's level of education, what they studied and see from that if it reveals anything about their ability to know the purchase and sale forms, and be able to effectively help you negotiate. Look at the writing in their personalized printed collateral that is included in the seller packet they give to you when you meet. Is it informative, can they convey information effectively? Check out their website, blog, brochure, information sheets. Ask them if they personally wrote that content. Many agents pay to have all written collateral done for them by a third party.

Short Sales and Foreclosures...

This is unfortunately a topic we have all heard about far too much in the past few years and hopefully as a home owner you are not facing this situation. A short sale is when the owner of a property is short the money needed to pay off their existing mortgage (loan) when they sell their house. For example, a seller purchased his house two years ago for $400,000 and now is being relocated and needs to sell. The current state of the market dictates that his list price should be $300,000. Thus, he is short $100,000, plus the sale fees and taxes involved in listing and selling a property. He does not have money on hand to make up the difference at closing. Thus when he lists his home, his agent will indicate that it is a short sale. This means if the seller gets a full price offer of $300,000, he must then negotiate with the lender (the holder of his mortgage) to forgive or write off all or a portion of the outstanding $100,000 he still owes. There are now short sale negotiators involved in these transactions, in addition to the agents and attorneys. Short sales can take many months after an offer is received to settle and they are not usually a buyer's first choice to purchase for that reason and because the seller's lender usually requires the buyer to not make offers on any other properties while they wait to hear back. If you are facing a short sale situation, it is best that you first consult with a local real estate attorney who handles short sales and you hire a listing agent and a short sale negotiator who are well versed in working short sales. You want to make sure when a buyer's offer is approved and the funds you are short are negotiated, that you are not left with an outstanding balance that you will still have to pay off or that a second lien holder cannot legally come after you to collect what you owe them. You need to verify that all the shortage, the outstanding mortgage/equity line of credit debt has been officially forgiven and get that in writing. Verify you are not going to be on the hook for some of that money down the line when you think you have settled free and clear.

Obviously, if your property has been foreclosed then you are not going to be selling your house but here is the definition just for clarity. Foreclosures are sales where the lender has actually repossessed a property and is now reselling it. A seller defaults on their mortgage, can no longer pay and is booted out of the property.

Sample Purchase and Sale Agreement...

Hopefully when you meet with a prospective listing agent they will provide you with a sample purchase and sale agreement to review ahead of time. This does not mean you have to become a forms expert, it is written by real estate attorneys after all! But you do need to have some idea what each page that you will be signing and/or initialing means. That is your name you are signing on each page and you are acknowledging your responsibility by signing. I think, the best time to for a seller to review the purchase and sale agreement information is ahead of time, before you have listed your house for sale. Your mind will be clearer and you will be more grounded. By reviewing this sample purchase and sale agreement, you will have a good of idea of what is coming later and hopefully a better understanding of what each page you sign actually means you are agreeing to do or not do. When you do get an offer, you will have reviewed the basic paperwork ahead of time so your level of confidence will be higher and your level of anxiety lower.

I have had clients take the sample purchase and sale agreement and then go meet with a real estate attorney to review it in detail, prior to listing their property. You may want to do that or you may want to have your purchase and sale agreement structured such that you are entitled to an attorney review period after mutual agreement is reached. Some states require real estate attorney reviews, Washington State does not. It is up to you to make this decision. Remember that the sample purchase and sale agreement that you review in advance, when you actually receive an offer, your purchase and sale agreement may have a few forms more or less than your sample packet contained. Each sale has its unique requirements. But at least the nuts and bolts of the purchase and sale agreement is in your sample packet and you have had a chance to become familiar with it in advance.

One thing I want to stress, if you have any questions that are of a legal nature, your real estate agent must refer you to a local real estate attorney for those answers. At no time is an agent permitted to answer a question of a legal nature. To do so, would be to practice law. Even if your agent knows 100% what the correct answer to your legal question is, she still should keep her mouth shut and refer you to a real estate attorney. This is also true for any tax and finance questions. You should be referred to appropriate professionals in that field who can best answer your questions. There is nothing worse than the know-it-all real estate agent. No one can know it all in this field. To have an ego that big is boring. It is also dangerous if clients are blindly following that agent's advice in areas they should not be commenting.

Response Time...

It is important when you are interviewing agents that you see how good they are with their response time. Do you receive the information they promised you on time? You need a real estate agent that promptly provides you and escrow with all the necessary signed around paperwork for your deal. You also need to judge how efficient your agent is up front because he will be the one delivering any offers to you. If your agent is lax, then you might not be getting offers right away as required by law. When you meet with prospective agents if they promise to get some additional information to you, do they deliver on time as promised; i.e. those additional sales comps or additional marketing information. If they are not doing this at the start of your working relationship with them, then that is probably a good indicator as to how things are going to go later. Later on, you are going to be more stressed, reviewing offers, a buyer's inspection, signing and closing, moving out, etc..., the last thing you want to have to stress about is if your unorganized listing agent is going to come through on things that need to be taken care of.

Estimated Seller's Net Proceeds...

The estimated seller's net proceeds is a fancy way of saying what you the seller are going to actually end up with in your bank account once all is said and done. The first word to be aware of is "estimated." It is not a guarantee and no agent can provide you with an absolute bottom line guaranteed net number. The estimation should however, be close to what you end up with. In my area where I sell, the standard estimation percentage is usually 9%. That includes the selling and listing office commissions, title and closing fees and taxes. It is actually sometimes a bit over the end result cost to the seller. However, I think it is better to try and over-estimate than under estimate! So you take the suggested list price and times that by the selling fee percentage and deduct that amount from the sale price, then deduct the remainder due on your mortgage to arrive at the approximate figure you the seller should be netting in the end. This net proceeds sheet is something a good listing agent is going to review with you when they are going over the list price suggestion. You should know prior to listing your property for sale, approximately what your net result is going to be if your home sells for list price.

Marketing Your Property...

One final topic to mention when you are vetting various listing agents is marketing. In my opinion, the best marketing exposure your property is going to get is via the MLS listing report. This is where all agents look for available properties and where the public now looks by default as most MLS listings are now available on a huge variety of privately run and public web sites. Most agents are going to send your listing to various independent websites as well, so in today's world you can rest assured your listing is going to be all over the web. The web is where the public is now first looking. This is why I am such a stickler for a listing agent filling out the listing paperwork properly, posting necessary documents online with their listing when it goes live, creating viable listing remarks/marketing verbiage, and taking the best photographs possible (more on this later). Most likely they will send out an e-flyer announcing your listing to other real estate agents touting your property. A listing agent may also send out mailers to surrounding properties to announce your listing or to their own marketing sphere.

Luxury Property…

With higher end properties a prospective agent may rave about the exclusive luxury property magazine they will advertise your property in. As someone who started out working for luxury real estate agents and has been involved in representing my own clients in that arena over the years, I have seen firsthand how this kind of luxury marketing goes. Typically, in my opinion, those ads are vanity ads. Yes, they look lovely and the available luxury properties magazine they are placed is usually mailed out to high income zip codes. That might not be as great as you think. Those in the high income zip codes who receive these publications are not usually looking to purchase another mansion, especially locally. Many listing agents tout these publications as something that should wow you. I would take it into consideration but know that these types of ads usually do not sell your property.

Those ads are however, great marketing exposure for your listing agent to land other high end listings and maybe get some high end buyers. This is not to say that sometimes these kinds of ads do not help promote a property but in my experience I have not seen a sale directly result from a luxury ad. Anyone who is in the market for a high end property, most likely will have the brains to have a good buyer's agent representing them from the very start of their search. They may tell their agent they noticed a particular ad in a luxury property magazine. Their buyer's agent then looks it up in the MLS. Their agent is also going to pull up all of the other available listings that match their buyer's criteria. The person shopping for a high end property is going to want to see the overview of what is available and then choose via the MLS search their agent does for them, what properties they want to see.

The main thing to look at if you are selling a high end property (or any property) is how competent and ethical a prospective listing agent is. Not who runs the most glossy high end property ads or who pulls in the driveway in the shiniest Bentley. Who can actually get the job done and be of the most value to you come negotiation time? Who can keep things organized and make sure your sale is handled properly and per the law? It is not in your wallet's best interest to base your listing decision solely on surface appearances, affected attitude, luxury ads or someone's Social Register status.

I can tell you that when I represent buyers who are looking at high end properties, quite a few of the listing agents in that arena have attitude for miles. Usually, I find that kind of snotty attitude is masking their deep insecurity. I think a high end seller is going to be best served by an agent who is truly competent and preferably attitude free. Over the years, I have had many buyers comment on the snotty and nasty attitude of high end listing agents. This does not impress the buyers and certainly does not help you the seller! Many luxury agents are competent and ethical, have nice personalities and interact like real professionals. That is what I would advise you seek if you are a high end seller.

Real Life...

A while back I represented a buyer who was purchasing a home. It was a real close choice between two houses; in fact he liked both of them almost equally. However, he decided to make an offer on one of them first and see how that played out and if that did not go well, he had a very close back up house he could make an offer on. I called the listing agent in the morning and let her know that my client and I were going to meet around 2 p.m. that day to write up an offer on her listing. I asked if there was anything the seller wanted us to know before writing up an offer. I also asked if the seller was in town/available as the offer would have a 9 p.m. expiration for that evening. Would she be able to meet with her seller in the early evening to review my buyer's offer? The listing agent said it would be no problem. I also let the listing agent know that my buyer had a very close second choice and he wanted the seller to know that (I also indicated that in the cover letter that I include with all of my buyer's offers). I got my buyer's offer done, with a 9 p.m. expiration, and sent it over to the listing agent (per her instructions) by 3:30 p.m. I called and left a message and emailed the listing agent to let her know the expected offer was there.

By 8:30 p.m. I had heard nothing back. So I called the listing agent and eventually reached her. She told me she was at a bar celebrating with her friends and they would have to look over the offer tomorrow. I reminded her that my client's offer expired at 9 p.m. that evening and that my client had a very close second choice. The listing agent became very annoyed with me, I guess because I interrupted her party time. She said, "*Well too bad because it is not happening tonight. We can just change the expiration on your client's offer tomorrow when I meet with the seller and show it to her and we should be good.*" I explained that was not the case, my client was going to be (rightfully) angry and that the law states she needed to get my client's offer to the seller tonight. The huffy agent replied, "*That's not going to happen, so just take the stick out of your ass and relax. We'll look it over tomorrow.*" And with that she hung up on me.

I immediately called and left a message with the listing agent's designated broker. I then called the seller's phone number indicated in the listing report form to see if I could meet with her directly since her agent was not doing her job. However, the number the listing agent had entered in the listing report for the seller was no longer in service. Mind you, this was not a seller's market and was in fact one of the strongest buyer's markets in a long time. Inventory was not selling fast and this house had been on the market for well over 90 days. More reason for the listing agent to be moving at the speed of lightening to get my buyer's offer in front of her seller.

I contacted my buyer and let him know what had occurred. He was angry. At 9 p.m. his offer expired. We met at 9:30 p.m. and he wrote up an offer for his second choice. I called that listing agent and we had his offer for his second choice set to expire the following day at noon. This listing agent knew how to do her job and by midnight, she had met with her seller and they had signed off on my buyer's offer and we had mutual agreement. The next morning at 9 a.m. my phone started ringing, the listing agent's designated broker called and the listing agent sent me an email letting me know she was going to meet with her seller later in the day to go over my client's (expired) offer. They had missed the boat due to the listing agent's negligence. Unfortunately, the seller had no way of knowing how much her agent had screwed her over. Legally I could not call the seller after the fact to let her know what had occurred, though I wanted to! Naturally the listing agent went into great theatrics over my client moving on to his second choice. It's always fun to watch how lazy or incompetent agents pitch huge fits when the whole problem is directly due to their gross negligence/laziness. I always say the louder they scream, the guiltier they are.

Long story short, I filed a complaint against this agent with the local MLS, she was not a member of the National Association of Realtors or I would have reported her there as well. It is too bad I legally could not let her seller know what had occurred, because the seller could most likely have sued the agent and her brokerage for

48

negligence. My client purchased a great house and that listing agent did a wonderful job. The other seller had her place languish on the market for a few more months before taking it off the market and renting it out. Hopefully this story shows you firsthand how important it is to trust the agent you choose to list your home with and how important it is for them to actually do their job. It is very difficult for you as a seller to know about these far too common situations that go on behind the scenes. I could literally write pages with these kinds of stories that I have personally encountered. Please take the time up front to choose the right person to represent you. It is really true in real estate that, *time is of the essence*!

THREE

MANIPULATION

The topic of manipulation is very pertinent when it comes to selling a home. The world of sales abounds with manipulators of all stripes. Some are natural born manipulators, others are trained to manipulate. Either way, in my opinion, it is not something that lends credibility to the real estate or lending professions and it is certainly why the generic term "sales" is so reviled in many circles. Please note, not all sales people are manipulators. The manipulator sales stereotype exists for a reason but if you are grounded and take the time to organize yourself up front, hopefully you can avoid those who do business by manipulating. Many manipulators are quite proud of their girls' club (I say girls' club not boys' club as most agents and loan people are female) and over the years the shop talk that I have overheard behind the scenes has curdled my ears! They boast of their manipulative abilities, their ability to "turn" a client, to essentially force their will/agenda on the unsuspecting client.

The public is equally to blame for this manipulative dynamic. Many sellers apparently love to have smoke blown at them, be cooed over, praised for their selling savvy, have their vanity and ego stroked and their home praised to the hilt, while their wallet is being emptied. It takes two to tango! If that is what you enjoy, have it. But you can be a responsible and informed seller and find someone to work with who is not always going to stroke your ego just to get the listing. You don't have to choose to work with someone who tells you only what you want to hear; i.e. that your swamp lands dump of a house is the next Hearst Castle, and you should be able to get top dollar for it.

Signs of Manipulation...

Here are some key signs that you might be dealing with a manipulative real estate agent.

1. The agent networks through family, friends, social clubs, religious institutions, and makes you feel obligated to work with them due to your common connection. This is similar to your coworker who is always chasing you down the hallway and popping into your office to try and sell you their latest multi-level marketing product. You know the skin creams, the time shares, the miracle life juice, etc...? They use your common connection and warp your friendship or familial status to essentially force you into using their real estate services. They usually have an aggressively pleasing personality but it is clear your friendship or connection with them is completely tied up in your supporting their business.

2. A friend, co-worker, boss, strongly pressures you to work with their real estate agent. This could be a sign the agent is providing them with a referral fee or a percentage of their commission from your sale. This is illegal in some states. In the many years I have taught classes, here is the worst story I have heard regarding this item. A woman attended the class after she had signed around her deal and she was set to close in a week. A condition of her loan was to

51

attend a certified home buyer class. When I got to this item in the class, the woman started crying. She then told the class that when she started to look into buying a house her boss called her in. He told her if she did not use X real estate agent to buy her house, then within 30 days of closing on her new place, he would find a legitimate reason to fire her. Obviously we were all stunned. This is the most blatant manipulative story I have heard, thus far. We asked her why she did not report this to her personnel director or better yet seek legal help. She felt it was best to not rock the boat and go along. Because she had poor boundaries and probably low self esteem, she allowed herself to get brow beat into using an agent she did not care for. I suspect she ended up purchasing something she was not that thrilled with either. Please do not let this happen to you in a selling capacity; i.e. if you don't use agent X to list and sell your house then your boss says he will find a reason to fire you once your home has sold.

3. The agent acts like they are your new best friend. They may take you to concerts, treat you to dinner, buy you gifts, anything to land you as a client. While that may feel flattering, it's manipulative. Find a new best friend somewhere else. This is business first, there is way too much money involved for it not to be. This is not the breezy, light and frothy, *are we having fun yet*, arena. Go find Barbie or Ken elsewhere if you are looking for that. It's

not to say you cannot have fun while selling your house or have a good connection with your agent. But again, this is something that requires attention to detail, experience, and for you to wear your grown up hat. Otherwise you might just skim the surface with Barbie or Ken and fun-time your way right into a deal you truly regret. Or you may overlook important steps/factors because you are too busy being dazzled and getting a natural high off having fun while selling your house.

4. The agent says they will pay you money (give you a discount) for listing with them. They may say they will pay (or refund) you money at closing or after closing. These situations can be illegal. Even if they are completely legit, do you really want to work with someone that is either so desperate or incompetent that they have to pay clients to work with them? Does your dentist, accountant, lawyer, etc…, pay you money to work with them? In my opinion, a good listing agent knows their worth and knows the services they are providing are worth the commission they are earning. The key word there is earning. They work hard and are good at what they do. Anyone who thinks being a real estate agent is a fun and easy job is gravely mistaken. Rewarding yes, fun at times, but easy, absolutely not. The old saying is true, *"10% of the agents do 90% of the work."* In my opinion, good agents do not need to pay or otherwise coerce people into working with them.

5. Agent does not provide you with active and sold comparison data sheets before you decide what your list price is going to be. Prior to the internet, manipulative agents used to brag about not giving their clients these comp sheets. Their theory was the more information you the seller had, the longer the time to get the listing, the more questions you might ask. Go figure. Slimy agents would get you to list your house for less than it was worth and then turn around and sell it to one of their buyers at the lower price they knew their client could afford. Yet another reason why dual agency is never a good idea. Now that more sales price information is available online, it is more difficult for agents to hide this information from you.

6. Agent does not provide you with an Estimated Seller's Net Proceeds sheet prior to listing and/or guarantees you will net a certain amount if you list with them.

7. An agent does not supply you with a sample purchase and sale agreement to read over prior to listing your property. As you know, I think it is best you receive this sample packet when you first meet with your agent. A good agent wants you to be informed, to ask questions and feel comfortable with what you are doing. Giving you a sample purchase and sale agreement to review in advance can help with this. A manipulator does not like it when you are informed or when you ask too many questions. They want to keep things light and airy and keep you moving along as

fast as possible. If you have time to think or ask questions then you may slow things down for them or worse yet, begin to see through their smoke and mirrors routine.

8. Watch out for the agent that is all personality, smiles and good times. They have charm and charisma and make you feel special, smart, appreciated and everything is always upbeat, sunshine and roses. These characteristics while nice sounding and sometimes fun to be around are usually the typical signs of a manipulator. It is the distinction between charm and manipulative driven sales versus character and informational driven sales. A good agent can have a nice personality/charisma but they also have substance/ethics. They provide you with good, unbiased information so you can make up your own mind about a property. They do not have an agenda or allow their ego to rule your sale. Someone with character does not always tell you (your ego) what you want to hear. That doesn't mean they are rude to you but they politely state the facts or their opinion and then let you decide what is best for you. I love the much touted word "integrity" which the sales world is so fond of using. If someone truly has integrity and works with integrity, they don't typically run around crowing about it every chance they get. Sort of like the old story about those who sing the loudest in church....

Sometimes I will get sellers who are suffering from what I call "seller-itis." For example, I went on a listing appointment a while back and before I had finished shaking the home owner's hand she wanted to know what I could get her for her house. I explained to her that I needed to first tour her house, go over the active and sold comps with her, review my seller packet with her and then if she was still interested, set up a time to go tour the area's like properties. Then we could see what a viable list price was and figure out her estimated seller's net proceeds sheet. She was not having any of this, it was strictly what are you going to get me; I don't have time for this other stuff. So I politely told her that I was not the person she would want to work with and left. Six months later she called me again. She had listed her house with an eager agent who told her what she wanted to hear and listed the place for a price way over what the current market said was reality. So it sat for six months. She fired her listing agent and was now starting over and interviewing agents again. I told her I would meet again if she was willing to take the time to do what I originally suggested. She did. I listed her house at a realistic price and it sold fairly soon thereafter.

Real Life...

As you already know, I am not a fan of dual agency. Years ago, I was contacted to meet with a potential seller for a listing appointment. I did my usual research and homework and met with the sellers. I toured their home and went over the active and sold comp data with them. I then explained that once they were firm on their agent choice, I would like to take them out on a tour to see similar active properties so they could see the competition in person and thus choose an appropriate list price. They thanked me and let me know they had one more agent they were interviewing and they would be in touch.

I heard from the sellers a couple of days later. They said they really liked what I had provided and really wanted to work with me. However, they had a fine line to walk as their niece just got her real estate license and wanted to list their house. I gave them my take on that and they pretty much already knew that would not be a wise choice for many reasons. They were going to use the line about keeping business and family separate and her newbie status was too risky for them, as this house was their nest egg. That resolved, they said that there was another agent they interviewed and he was the "specialist" for their neighborhood. They were not completely thrilled with him. They found him very pushy and some of the neighbors did not have a great opinion about him. But, he had told them he could make sure their place sold in 30 days and that they would get list price/top dollar for them and discount his commission.

I asked the sellers how this was possible. They said this agent told them that he had an interested buyer for their home and at the list price he suggested, he could put this deal together. Sounded good on the surface I suppose. But, this agent was proposing a dual agency deal, whereby he would represent the sellers and the buyer and collect both commissions. The sellers already knew I did not think that was in their best interest. I then asked how the list price he proposed for their house was arrived at. He had not provided them with comparison data and had merely quoted them a figure. He said was the neighborhood specialist and so he knew what list prices worked and did not work.

I told the sellers that I really could not comment on this agent or the information he provided them. I would love to work with them, they knew my way of doing business, and they would have to make up their minds on their own.

They ended up listing with Mr. Neighborhood Specialist and he promptly sold their house to his buyer within less than a day of the listing going live. Turns out the list price he had the sellers agree to was under what I had suggested their list price range should be and what the current state of the market data indicated was correct. My list price range was based on the sold comp data and other current listings. I strongly suspect his list price was based on what his buyer could afford to pay.

Months later, I listed a house down the street from where these sellers had lived and it was listed for an amount that fell in the same range as I had provided the other people with. This house sold within a couple of weeks and went for the list price. While removing my key box from this listing, the former owners of the house Mr. Neighborhood Specialist sold, happened to see me while driving by. They stopped and filled me in on their experience. They regretted listing with the neighborhood specialist agent and felt he had undersold them. They were not happy they had agreed to let him be a dual agent, and told me they wished they had listened to their better judgment and not to his smoke and mirrors. I had to politely nod and tell them I was sorry things had not worked out to their liking. I did end up getting a referral from those folks so that was nice. This story shows you how manipulators can work to get listings and unfortunately this type of story is far too common. Hopefully, you will take heed and make sure you are completely comfortable with an agent before you agree to list your house for sale with them.

FOUR

PRE-LISTING

To recap what I suggest you do before you list your house for sale, you have:

1. Taken time to sit down and figure out your motivation for selling and what your ideal timeline is for selling.

2. You have reviewed your existing mortgage, equity lines of credit and know approximately what your break even sale price needs to be.

3. Chosen a real estate agent to represent you.

4. Reviewed the seller packet materials including the sample purchase and sale agreement and asked any questions that you may have.

5. Made sure you have funds in your checking account to cover miscellaneous out-of-pocket expenses (possible inspection repair requests, preliminary title fee, any condo resale certificate fees).

6. You have reviewed sales price scenarios and are certain you are not in a short sale situation; will not have to list the house as a short sale. Note here, sometimes people sell their house for less than they paid for it but it is not a technical short sales (does not have to be listed as such) because the owner has enough cash to make up the shortage due at closing.

7. Reviewed an estimated seller's net proceeds sheet based on the suggested list price and have determined you are okay with the estimated net figure that is outlined.

8. Studied active and sold comps and have arrived at a list price that both you and your listing agent think is realistic and a good price point.

Repairs…

Now you are ready to meet with your listing agent and go over all of the pre-listing items that need to be taken care of before your house actually goes on the market for sale. A good agent is going to have a checklist of items to review with you and hopefully they have some notes from when they originally toured your house with you. It is usually in your best interest to have your house as show ready as possible when you list it. The better is shows the better offer you will hopefully receive. One of my biggest pet peeves when I am working as a buyer's agent is when I am trying to show a listing and the key sticks in the lock, the door is difficult to open, etc…. I hate listing reports where the listing agent states, *"Key sticks in lock, just be patient and jiggle it until it opens."* Novel idea, why not address that annoying issue prior to listing the property? It is a pain for agents who are trying to show the property and it means the buyer sits there on the front steps waiting while their agent tries to unlock the house. Subconsciously, the buyer already has a mental notion that this house is "defective" the lock doesn't work properly, what else is wrong with this place? The seller must be a lax owner who does not take care of maintenance. Not a great first impression for a potential buyer and not a good way for you to get top dollar for your property. This might seem like a simple and even a silly item, but I encounter this at least once a week. I hear buyers comment on stuck locks all the time and they always semi jokingly ask what else is wrong with the house. Worse yet, sometimes there are places where despite the buyer and me both trying, we cannot get the door to open, so we don't tour the place. Quite often the buyer just marks the house we can't get into off their list of potentials. Thus, the seller has lost out on a potential buyer because of a lock that sticks!

Another example of shoddy listing work, I took clients to tour a house a while back. First, the photos posted online were awful, we'll take more about photos in a bit. But when showing, it took us quite a while to locate the key box. It had not been secured to the front door handle and there was no indication in the listing report as to where the electronic key box could be found. We eventually found it in the back yard, secured to the rear fence post behind the garden shed. That's a real intuitive location, wouldn't you say?! Once we had the keys, it took us about fifteen minutes to trick the old lock to open for us. Once in, the hallway lights were burned out, the initial impression was a dark space. In the kitchen the handle to the oven was broken off (something that could easily be replaced for not a lot of money). The carpets were stained and smelled bad; having carpets cleaned prior to listing is not rocket science! A few small panes in various windows were cracked and needed replacing, my clients noted the master bath's toilet handle was broken and the rear deck's railing was missing spokes and on its last leg. In fact, the listing agent noted in the listing remarks, to beware of the deck's weak railing. This was not a short sale or foreclosed property and it was in a nice area. The list price was in the fair market value range.

When my clients decided to make an offer on this house, they could not get all of these small repairable items out of their minds. Consequently they felt justified offering ten thousand dollars less than the list price. They noted other properties listed in the area did not have all of these annoying needed repair items. Had the listing agent insisted on the seller fixing these items prior to listing, the seller most likely would have gotten a full list price offer. All said, these various repair items probably would have cost a few thousand dollars tops to address prior to listing. This hopefully shows you how repair items can come back to haunt you come offer time and how buyers do take note of these things and offer accordingly. Please pay attention to items your agent suggests you should repair prior to listing, they can literally make or break your chances of getting top dollar for your house.

A few years ago I had a seller who could easily have been on a hoarders show on TV. I let her know in order to get her house sold and for top dollar she was going to need help addressing her situation. I arranged to have a hoarding specialist meet with her and I provided them with my long list of items I needed to have taken care of before I could even think of listing her place. One year later they were done and it was unreal how much she had cleared out of her house, it was a completely different place. I asked her if she now wanted to stay in the house and not sell since it was now so nice! She wanted to list and move on and hopefully start a new life free of hoarding. She got her asking price and as far as I know is still in her new home and no longer hoarding.

Staging…

Next up is staging. I always say when staging your house for sale that you need to make it, *"nice but neutral."* Neutral is usually somewhat boring and not very fun to live in but in terms of selling that is what is going to help you. This does not necessarily mean hiring one of the popular staging companies to come in and literally stage your house. There are times when these companies can be quite helpful but it depends on the market and your unique situation. A good listing agent can help you prep or stage your house prior to listing. Please do not be insulted if she comes with a list of items to address in order to get your space listing ready. It is not meant to be insulting to you, it is meant to help you get the most money you can in the shortest amount of time. Do not be ashamed if you have closets that are bursting at the seams, a broken screen door, etc…, your agent will most likely have seen it all and worse! The main thing is that you take action before your house goes on the market to make it look as good as it possibly can. Every seller who is smart does some kind of staging on their home before listing. Even if you are Martha Stewart perfect, there are still certain items to address prior to listing.

The most common item is to clear out closets, the garage, basement and attic. You want these spaces as open and as orderly as possible. If you are someone who crams things in closets, it's time to unpack them. You can have a yard sale or put these items in a storage unit. In fact, renting a storage unit to hold things until your place sells is often a great idea. There may be large pieces of furniture that your agent thinks would best be removed prior to listing, so your rooms appear larger or flow better. Your agent may suggest rearranging furniture. Please do not be offended, it is not intended to be a dig at your home's décor or your design sense. A good listing agent is going to be up on what the public is clicking with and know how to make your rooms appear more buyer-friendly. This quite often means removing items or rearranging them. Your whole house is basically being transformed into a showroom; a showroom that quite frankly, most people find difficult to actually live in day to day. Transforming your space into a showroom or magazine spread of sorts hopefully means more money for you and less time on the market.

De-cluttering countertops, removing family photos is also a common task. I like for clients to neutralize their house so the buyer can envision themselves living there and not get hung up on who is actually is living there. This means removing religious or spiritual icons, out go the cross, Buddha statues, crystals, etc.... It's nothing personal; you just do not want a prospective buyer to focus on those items. Remove any books, DVDs that might be considered controversial or give a strong indication as to who you the seller are, and take down the personal photos. Remove all items from the front of your refrigerator and clear off the kitchen counter tops! Is your shower filled with eight bottles of different shampoos, take them out. Is your dining room table currently being used as a "temporary" desk, clear it off. Is the pantry overflowing with old plastic bags and its shelves crammed with hundreds of canned goods, out they go.

If you have children or teenagers you have an additional hurdle. At a minimum, try and have your children confine their toys and personal clutter to their rooms. Buyers are a bit more forgiving if a child's room appears a bit junky. But the child's room should still be navigable. This is not easy, especially if you have small children who play with their Lego and toy cars in the living room. I suggest you try and make preparing for a showing appointment a game with your child. Maybe even go out with your child and purchase a special plastic bin where all the toys that are out on the floor go when it is time for Mom or Dad to show the house. Make them think preparing for a showing is a race, a game of beat the clock; often it really is!

Another **tip** when staging, please do not try and cover up a material defect of any kind. This would be the hole in the living room wall that you place the sofa in front of to hide. Or perhaps the wall to wall carpeting is stained beyond repair, so you put an area rug on top of it to hide it. This will only come back to haunt you. Have this repair work done prior to listing or go ahead and show these defects and let your agent and any prospective buyer know they are there.

For example, a few years ago I had buyers who put in an offer on a condo and reached mutual agreement with the seller. Seemed like a great place and their inspection was going well. During the inspection, the buyers decided to lift up the area rug in the living room that was placed over the grey wall to wall carpeting in the center of the room. Sure enough, the carpeting underneath the area rug was burned in part and severely stained. The wall to wall carpeting needed to be replaced. Clearly the seller thought not disclosing this fact and covering it with an area rug until they moved out was good enough. Wrong! My buyers were so freaked by this discovery that they terminated the deal. Might be a bit of an overreaction but who could blame them? The seller disclosure statement that the seller filled out did not mention this known defect in the carpeting. What else were the sellers not disclosing or hiding? We couldn't look behind every piece of furniture, pull up every area rug, so what else was not okay? Had the sellers noted this in their disclosure statement or not covered up the carpeting defect, all probably would have gone well. Better yet, the seller should have replaced the carpeting prior to listing. Good example of how trying to trick someone or not wanting to fix something prior to listing can come back and cost you a deal. Please do not try and trick anyone and hide any known defects!

Cleaning...

If you keep your house so clean you can eat dinner off the floor, this section is not for you. Real estate agents love sellers who keep their homes, "*scary clean.*" Clearly, cleaning is not going to be something you need to worry about if you fall in this category. However, most of us are going to have to put some effort into pre-cleaning and then daily cleaning while the house is on the market. This is where many sellers get frustrated. Once you have de-cluttered your space, it might be time to have the carpets professionally cleaned, repaint walls, have a maid service come in and scour the mold and mildew out of your shower, have the window screens removed and all windows cleaned inside and out, empty out the refrigerator and clean it from top to bottom, including the freezer. You name it, clean it! If you hate cleaning and you can afford it, hire someone else to do it for you. Otherwise, grin and bear it and get to work. Make this your mantra while cleaning, "*top, dollar, top dollar….*" Places that are clean, show well and sell faster, period. Make sure all burned out light bulbs are replaced. You and your agent can talk about adding wattage to make rooms appear lighter, putting lamps in dark corners, etc.…

Go ahead and have the windows professionally washed inside and out, you might be amazed how much better that makes your house look. Make sure all showers and bath tubs are sparkling clean, buyers definitely look and take note of moldy showers and tubs. Make sure your oven is cleaned and not coated in baked on grease, buyers look in the oven and ditto for your freezer, no frozen goo or a clogged up ice bin. The washer and dryer should also be sparkly on the outside and not full of lint and debris inside.

Another thing to review before listing is the odor of your house. All houses have odors, some better than others. Typically you the owner cannot really smell the odor in your own home because you live there and are accustomed to it. Do not freak out if your listing agent politely tells you that your house smells bad or is "stuffy." Be thankful. I have a nose like a scent hound and when I am touring with clients, the odor of the house is the first thing I notice. Do I smell mold, where's that smelly litter box, what is that musty dust odor? Synthetic plug-in air fresheners are not your friend. Many buyers and agents are allergic to them and to me they are usually way too strong and they make me wonder what odor the sellers are attempting to cover up; i.e. is there a mold issue with this property? This is also true of the synthetically scented candles which were more popular prior to the plug-in invasion.

What to do if you are a smoker and have smoked inside your place? Don't fool yourself; everyone can smell it a mile away. If it is a serious, years-old smoke odor and your walls are nicotine stained, then it is time to go buy the odor cover sealer paint at your hardware store. This product is used in houses that have caught on fire and have heavy smoke residue in them. You will need to paint every room, ceilings included, in this product and sometimes it takes several coats. Then paint over that sealer product with regular wall paint. If you have wall to wall carpeting, that also probably needs to be replaced. Also, if you plan to still occupy your house after doing all of this de-smoking work, then you will need to only smoke outside and far from the house. Make sure your butts go in a coffee can that you hide. I have had smoker clients do this work and then decide to move out and live elsewhere while their house is on the market so they can continue with their smoking and not adversely affect their sale potential.

If you are someone who uses a lot of perfume every day, then you might want to start sprit-zing yourself outside so the fumes do not linger and a potential buyer starts breaking out in a round of sneezes when touring your house. If there is a litter box, pet bunny or other inside critter you need to make sure their litter box and living area is kept clean at all times. Another note, if you have a dog and you let them use your back yard as their litter box, make sure you clean up after them. Nothing annoys buyers more than to tour a house and then walk around the back yard only to step on one of your pooch's land mines!

Then there is the garbage. Please take your garbage out daily while your house is on the market, you do not want a buyer focusing on a garbage odor while in your house. Same for making sure your refrigerator is free of green slime items while listed. If you cook a lot at home, good for you for eating healthy. However, make sure you air out the house after each meal you prepare. If you always eat take-out and fast food, throw those boxes and bags away outside every day and air the house out. You do not want your house smelling like a fast food chain or a restaurant that specializes in curry dishes, corned beef and cabbage, etc.... You want to make sure your house smells clean, fresh and a buyer is not immediately distracted by any odor, good or bad. I also recommend my clients open the windows daily and air their house out.

You and your agent can also discuss other staging items that are specific to your property. If your house is dark, then increase the bulb wattage, add lamps. You may want to play quiet music in the background. Just make sure if you do play music that it is bland. No rap or country; actually think classical or quiet jazz and always at a low volume so it is not distracting. Fresh flowers are always nice but that routine can get real old and expensive if your house is on the market for a while. So you may want to explore some indoor potted plants or maybe artificial plants that appear real. Some agents like to have their sellers set the dining room table for showings. I am indifferent to that one, if you want to do that it won't hurt but I am not sure it really adds anything. If your place is a vacant listing, your agent may have you put in a few staging items. However, please do not leave a bowl of fresh apples on a table or fresh flowers unless you plan to check on them and replace them every couple of days. A while back I showed a vacant property that had a bowl of rotting apples on the entry table with maggots in them! That certainly was not appealing to the buyers and distracted them.

Your agent should provide you with a cheat sheet list of items to take care of before any showings or before you leave your house for work. This daily fire drill would include such things as removing the garbage, turning on the lights that you and your agent determined need to be left on, turning on music, cleaning out the sink, making up the bed, putting the dirty laundry away, vacuuming, airing out the place, opening or closing blinds in certain rooms, etc....

The last thing I want to add for staging is for lack of a better term, selling voodoo. Over the years I have had all kinds of sellers that I have worked with. Some have their priest come out and bless their house before listing, dig a hole in the yard and bury a St. Joseph statue or bury certain mineral stones for good selling juju. I have had energy clearers and psychic visits homes to clear them, shamans come and perform rituals, smudge the rooms, you name it I think I have seen it. Whatever works for you is great and I am big believer in doing anything that might help sell a house faster. I know firsthand that each house has its own unique energy or feeling. Some energy is more welcoming than others. Whatever it takes to make your house feel better and show better, I am all for it! So do not be shy about talking

71

with your real estate agent about this topic. We might laugh and call it voodoo but in reality the feeling or energy that a house gives off is a very real thing.

You can see this is no walk in the park and anyone who tells you that listing your house for sale is fun, is insane. But to get top dollar and an offer as soon as possible, these are the necessary steps you will need to take. Try to grin and bear it.

Does Not Convey...

When a listing agent takes a listing he will hopefully ask you if there is anything you intend to take with you (besides your personal belongings) when you move. You might say you are taking the dining room chandelier or the gnome statues in the back yard with you when you move.

The chandelier is an attached item and would not be considered personal property. Personal property is usually defined as anything that is not permanently affixed to the land; movable property. Prior to taking a listing a good listing agent will first try and convince the seller to go ahead and replace the chandelier. As in remove the chandelier they intend to take and buy and install another one. This keeps things very simple and no one gets fixated on the chandelier (yes there have been stubborn deals where each side demanded the chandelier or the deal was off). However, some sellers will not agree to replace the chandelier prior to listing. So, their listing agent should make a note in the listing report that the chandelier, *"does not convey"* or *"is not included"* or *"sellers are keeping the dining room chandelier,"* etc.... A smart listing agent is going to also insist that you hang a sign from the chandelier

72

noting once again this item stays with you the seller. A good listing agent will make sure this item is noted in the signed around purchase and sale agreement, that way there is no room for confusion. The buyer's agent may write in that the seller agrees to replace said chandelier with one of equal style/value or seller to install a specific chandelier the buyer wants, including the name and model number of the buyer's preferred chandelier. You can see, it is easier if you go ahead and remove and replace the chandelier prior to listing your house. This way there is no potential for a battle over a chandelier.

You would do the exact same thing if there is a rose bush planted in the yard that you intend to dig up and take with you when you move out. Again, it should be noted in the listing report, in your signed around deal and the rose bush should be clearly identified so the buyer knows in advance which specific bush is being taken away. Please do not take any other in-ground plants with you when you move, unless they are all clearly documented in your deal. Buyers do notice when sellers do this and many a times a seller has had to replant or replace the plants they should not have taken with them.

Those Pesky Gnomes...

The garden gnome statues are another matter. Technically they are considered personal property as they are not permanently attached to the house or land. There has been many a hissy fit over missing yard gnomes! A good listing agent is going to ask you in advance if you intend to take the yard gnomes when you move. Even though they are personal property, your agent may think it best to pack them up prior to listing or he may want to make a special note reminding the buyer they do not stay. Technically that is not necessary but to avoid any misunderstandings sometimes it is best to note it. Some other examples of seller's personal property that is usually outdoors are: birdbaths, portable storage sheds or play houses that are not permanently attached to the land via a slab foundation, firewood, moveable outdoor grills, any potted plants, swing sets or play equipment unless they are installed in-ground via cement.   If you do leave the garden gnome statues, then the buyer wins the gnome statue lottery!

Appliances...

The purchase and sale agreement has boxes to check off for appliances that are included in the sale of the property (in WA State). The listing report that your agent fills out should clearly indicate what appliances are included with the sale and which ones are excluded. Appliances mostly fall under the category of personal property as they can be removed (are not usually permanently attached). Lenders do not allow a mortgage to include personal property; they are only loaning money for real property (more on this next). However, lenders make an exception for appliances unlike the motor boat in the forthcoming example. The appliances are items that the seller can decide to take with them and sometimes you will see a listing where only the range/oven is being left. The rest of the appliances are being removed by the seller. This practice of the seller taking some or all of the appliances with them when they move is more common in some states than others. Per the buyer's specific loan type and any applicable regional or county appraisal rules for say FHA loans, lenders are going to usually require there be an operational stove/range and kitchen sink in order for the property to pass appraisal. Please make sure that your listing paperwork clearly states the appliances that you are leaving. Also note, you cannot randomly change your mind about which appliances you are taking or leaving. Especially once you have a signed around deal, the appliances you have indicated are staying must stay, zero exceptions. You cannot suddenly decide you are going to take the range/oven and replace it with a like kind prior to closing. This greatly upsets deals. You will have to prove what "like kind" is and get the buyer's written permission before doing this. A major pain, so figure all of this out before you list your property for sale and stick with exactly what your listing report and deal states. Otherwise you are entering the legal action realm.

Real Property Only…

Your listing agent should not include in your listing report an itemized list of personal items you wish to sell to a prospective buyer. For example, a listing agent should not advertise that included in the sale of your lake house is your motor boat or worse yet include this verbiage in your listing report or on marketing flyers, *"Free motor boat with full price offer."* The lake house and land (real property) are what the buyer's lender is loaning them money for and what the purchase and sale agreement covers. The motor boat is considered personal property belonging to you the seller. It should not be included in your listing or your purchase and sale agreement. The MLS rules in many areas forbid a listing agent to include offers of personal property in the listing report. Purchase and sale agreements are usually not supposed to include personal property, just real property. How would this motor boat conveyance work then?

You would have your listing agent let the buyer's agent know that you are also giving the buyer the motor boat if the offer is full price. If the buyer has interest in the motor boat, then a separate agreement, apart from the sale of your lake house, needs to be written up and agreed to by you and the buyer. Including personal property in your purchase and sale agreement will upset the buyer's lender, they view that as a monetary gain for the buyer and they are not lending the buyer money to purchase personal items (again appliances are an exception).

Another way this comes up is when the seller has a list of furnishings that are for sale. The seller says a buyer can purchase the dining room set for $1,500. If the buyer wants the dining room set, then they should make their offer for the house and get that agreed to. Then you and the buyer can work out the purchase of the dining room set on your own. The buyer's offer should <u>not</u> state something like, "*$320,000 purchase price including the seller's dining room set.*" or include verbiage on an addendum, "*Seller agrees to leave dining room set upon receipt of $1,500 from buyer at or on closing.*"

What about having your listing agent state that the offer price is $350,000 vacant or $375,000 including furnishings? Again, those personal items, "furnishings" need to be negotiated and paid for in a separate agreement between you and the buyer, without your real estate agent's involvement. A lender is not going to allow the buyer's mortgage to include $25,000 for furnishings. You would want the buyer to make an offer for the vacant property and then broker the sale of the furnishings separately without your agent's involvement. Here is a **tip**, if you are selling a furnished house, make sure you include a complete itemized and visual list of all included furnishing in the transfer of personal property agreement that you and the buyer sign. You should have an attorney assist you with this personal property agreement and help facilitate the verification of furnishings and payment.

Here is a story I heard recently, where a listing report stated that the seller would replace the old carpeting with new carpeting (the color choice made by the buyer) prior to closing. This was not indicated in the purchase and sale agreement paperwork and the loan person had no knowledge the carpet was being replaced with new carpeting in a color the buyer chose. When the deal went for the final underwriter review, apparently the underwriter reviewed the listing report and red flagged it. They requested the seller and buyer both sign a statement which stated the carpeting in this property had not been replaced by the seller per the buyer's selection of color. If they signed that, then they were technically lying and would be committing loan fraud. The underwriter then required the seller to provide the receipt for the new carpeting and made the loan person add that amount to the buyer's income/assets. It screwed up the loan terms as the buyer then showed more assets than worked for his loan requirements. On the surface allowing a buyer to choose the color of new carpeting sounds like a great idea and a win-win for everyone. This story shows how even good seller intentions can screw up deals. Ironically, if the seller had replaced the carpeting prior to listing and not allowed a buyer to choose the color they preferred, all would be good with the lender.

One last point, what if at some point after mutual agreement, you decide you do not want your sofa and would like to leave it, free of charge, for the buyer if they want it. Typically your agent can convey that message to the buyer's agent. If the buyer wants the sofa then you can leave it when you move out. But if the buyer does not want your free sofa, then you must remove it by the closing day. This all might sound petty and trivial, welcome to the wonderful world of residential real estate! The devil is literally in the details. Therefore, keep it simple and do not mix real property and personal property transactions and if in doubt spell it all out in writing with a local real estate attorney's help.

Photographs...

In today's market there is nothing worse for a seller of a property than having bad pictures of their property posted online. I am amazed at the number of active listings I run across every week online, that have horrible photographs. Almost all buyers are now online previewing listings themselves and they do this by scrolling through each listing's photographs. If the pictures posted online of your property are not good, then you are going to miss out on potential buyers and your place is going to take longer to sell. Many times I have found a great place for one of my buyer clients because the photos posted online for the listing are so awful no one has bothered to even take a look at the listing. I still do old school, in person, previewing so I have been able to find properties that appear terrible online but in person are actually really great places. My buyers benefit from this and they often comment on why any seller would list their property with an agent that does not take and post quality photographs.

Not all places are easy to photograph, some are downright hard. But every property can still be photographed to show its best potential. One great upper end house I came across recently, the main photo that pulled up online for all prospective buyers and agents to see was of the garage doors. How stupid is that! The house itself was magazine spread quality and the listing agent had put a shot of the very bland garage doors as her lead photo? Talk about costing the seller time and money! In my opinion, there is really no excuse for this. Then there are listings where the listing agent will post just one photo of the property or they only photograph the exterior or the view from the property. This automatically makes anyone viewing the listing think the house must be really ugly or a wreck because there are no good exterior shots and zero interior photos. I know as a buyer's agent this is not always the case. Many a time, I have previewed for a buyer and gone to one of these exterior only photo listings expecting to find a garbage dump of an interior and been completely wrong. Inside is a terrific place or at least a place that shows well and is clean. Why has their listing agent not taken the time to shoot photos of the interior and post them? Even if the inside is a total dump (the seller should have read my previous tips here) the listing agent should still take a couple of interior photos so people have a general idea of what's in store for them inside this listing. Posting nothing, yields nothing; buyers do not usually want to see it.

CHARLES CHAPLIN

For certain properties your listing agent may want to hire a professional photographer to take pictures of your house. With today's ever improving cameras, even phone cameras, anyone with half a brain can shoot half way decent photos of your house. You the seller want to review and approve these photos your agent takes to post online and put on marketing flyers. Some agents take lousy photos. The camera is turned sideways, a counter top juts into the photo frame, the lights are not turned on and it appears dark, there is dirty laundry or other junk lying on the floors in the photos, etc.... If a seller is not motivated to straighten up prior to having their house photographed for listing, how awful is it going to be when actual buyers are touring it?

A good listing agent should advise against this and require the seller clean up first and then shoot quality photos of the house that show it in its best possible light. I caution against using the wide angle or fish eye lenses to make rooms appear larger. Buyers can see that when they are looking online and they immediately notice it when touring. Subconsciously or consciously, they then start to think, the photos were deceptive so what else is being hidden or manipulated around here? I could write for pages how amazing it is to me the poor quality photos I see online for listings. It does not serve you the seller well and you should never let it happen. I hear listing agents comment, *"Well it's a seller's market so who really cares about the photos or how clean the house is, because everything is selling quickly now."* Nothing could be lazier or more incorrect in my opinion. Even if listings are selling overnight, having the place look good and having quality photos only serves the seller's best interest. The better it looks, the more offers will come in if it is a multiple offer scenario. In my opinion there is no excuse for poor photos or a lack of photos.

Ordering Title...

A good listing agent is going to have you choose a title company and then get preliminary title for your property ordered and ready to go when your listings goes live. If you do not know of or have a title company that you want to use, then ask your agent as he probably has one he likes working with. As a seller you are going to need to pay the fee upfront to pull the preliminary title report. Your agent will probably collect a check from you or have you mail it to the title company to cover this; usually it is about $50. Title companies charge around that amount to pull preliminary title for your property. If you decide a week or so after listing or months later, that you no longer want to sell your house then the title company will keep this fee as compensation for the work they did to pull the preliminary title report for you. If you get an offer and your house sells, then this fee will be credited toward the total amount you owe the title company at closing.

Title Insurance...

Title insurance protects against future losses resulting from past events. Traditionally, the title insurance company is chosen by the seller when they list their property and the buyer then chooses an escrow company when making an offer. The seller pays for the title company to guarantee clear title so the property can be sold and the deed recorded in the buyer's name. The buyer usually pays a title insurance premium for their lender. When a listing agent takes a listing, a good one will have a title company pull preliminary title and indicate that title company's name and the preliminary title report number in his listing. The buyer's agent then can write in that title company's name in the buyer's offer.

When I am working with a buyer and I run across a listing where the listing agent has not pulled preliminary title, I start to wonder what the problem is. Is there an issue with who really owns the property, is there a cloud on the title, is the listing agent completely clueless and doesn't know title needs to be pulled (not that uncommon unfortunately), etc...? Sometimes when the title company really starts to dig and verify things (after an offer is mutually accepted) they will discover hidden issues with the seller or the property, a cloud on the title that has to be cleared in order for the sale to close.

The title insurance company is going to verify the title is clear and that the person who says they are the owner is in fact legitimate and can actually sell the property. They will verify that there are no outstanding liens, warrants, judgments against you the seller/the property and will do the same for the buyer once you have a mutually agreed upon deal.

The title company will send you a preliminary title commitment either by email or by snail mail. You should read it over (even though it can be a bit dull) and contact the title representative with any questions you may have. It is going to list any known easements on the property. An easement example would be the power company's line that runs across the property. They will list the right of the power company to access the property to repair or do work on the power line that runs across your property. There may be unused easements. For example, my property has a railroad easement running across the back of it. It was recorded in the late 1800s and it is unused; in fact the railroad was never built. But in theory, the railroad still has their easement/access to the back of my lot.

The title report will list your name as the seller and most likely state they are investigating to confirm you are who you say you are and not someone with outstanding warrants, judgments against you. If you have a more common name like Bob Jones, then the report will probably state there are several outstanding issues with "Bob Jones" and they are investigating. That is because your name is common and besides you, the fine upstanding citizen Bob Jones, there are others out there with the same name as you, who are trying very hard to make their appearance on *America's Most Wanted*. When sellers first see that their name needs investigating by the title company they naturally freak. You can contact the title representative with any questions and for reassurance. You will see by the final title report that your name has been cleared and they will state there are no known issues with you.

There are also different types of title insurance and if you want to know more about the different types and what they cover and do not cover, then it is best to speak directly with the title company representative and let them fill you in on the various types, and reasons for them. Sometimes a buyer may have a question about a property line or need to know exactly where the official property boundaries are. Their agent can request (at the buyer's expense and it is not cheap) for the title company to do an extended report. This will entail hiring a surveyor to go out and physically survey and stake the property. Many sellers do not even glance at the title information that is sent to them but I encourage all sellers to review it and again contact the title representative directly with any title questions.

A good buyer's agent is going to include a Title Contingency Addendum Form 22T (in WA State) with their client's offer. If filled out correctly, this addendum entitles the buyer to review the preliminary title report for five days (usually) upon receipt. During that review time the buyer can note any exceptions that are listed and if they give you written notice of disapproval of the exceptions noted, then you the seller have a time period (usually five days) to give written notice to the buyer that you will correct all the disapproved exceptions before the closing date. If you do not provide written notice that you will clear the disapproved exceptions within the stated response time, then the buyer can terminate the deal and get their earnest money deposit returned (more on earnest money later).

Another note, many times the title company has an escrow division and your agent might want to indicate that the seller prefers to use the title company to also act as the escrow company for this transaction. Typically, bundling title and escrow can result in a price reduction for those services. But note, traditionally the buyer indicates in their offer the escrow company they would like to use; more on escrow later.

Seller Disclosure...

In Washington State, a Seller Disclosure Statement, Form 17, is usually provided by the seller (most states have or require a similar seller disclosure statement, check to see what is required in your state). A good listing agent will have this form posted with the listing on the MLS so that buyers and their agents have quick and easy access to it. When I am working with a buyer and this form is not posted online, I always ask the listing agent to send it over. Sometimes they will not respond, and other times they may say the seller has not filled it out yet. I always find that strange, especially if the property has been on the market for a few days or more. Why hasn't the seller filled out this form yet, are they trying to hide something? Is the listing agent forgetful and did not remember to have the seller fill it out, what's the story? This form is currently five pages long (in WA State) and it has questions about the condition of the property, environmental questions, age of property, etc.... The seller has the option of answering *"yes, no, don't know."* If you answer yes to any question that has an asterisk, then a written explanation needs to be provided.

When I work as a buyer's agent, I can tell you this form is almost always an issue. It is either not prepared so it cannot be reviewed in advance or it is filled out incorrectly; seller signature/initials are missing, questions are skipped that need to be answered, no written explanation provided where required, an out-of-date version of the form has been used, etc.... I never advise my buyer sign off on this form until it is completed in full by the seller on the most recent version. Usually I have to send back a list of items to the listing agent asking them to have the seller correct/answer or have them fill out the most current version of this form. I always tell my buyers if they receive a seller disclosure statement and it is completely filled out and has detailed written explanations where required and maybe even some additional repair information attached to it, that could actually be a good sign. A seller that is that thorough is probably someone who has stayed on top of things in terms of maintaining their home.

In WA State, the buyer can sign off on the seller disclosure statement such that they have waived their right to terminate the deal based on receipt of this seller disclosure review. Or they can sign such that they then have three days, after receipt, to review the seller disclosure, ask questions and terminate the deal based on not liking what they find in the disclosure. I do not advise my buyers to sign off such that the disclosure statement review period is waived upon receipt, unless it is a multiple offer scenario.

Please note that the information provided here for the seller disclosure statement is related to WA State practices. Your state may handle this statement differently or have different laws/requirements. There are times when a Seller Disclosure Statement, Form 17 is not required. One would be if the property is an estate sale. Fran's mother owned and lived in the house and she passed away. Fran inherited her mother's house. Fran, the estate, is not required to provide a seller disclosure statement to a buyer. Foreclosure sales (bank owned properties) are not going to provide a seller disclosure statement. For a while, new construction developers were not filling out the standard seller disclosure statement but were incorporating it (or a version of it) in their required builder addendum forms. Now, most new construction projects are providing the standard seller disclosure statement and are no longer incorporating them in their builder addendums.

Sometime a listing agent will say that the seller disclosure statement is not being provided because his seller is selling the property *"as is."* That holds no legal merit. *"As is"* does not magically remove a seller's liability or their obligation to provide a seller disclosure statement when required. Other times a landlord, who rents out a property but has never lived in it, will say they are not required to provide a buyer with a seller disclosure statement. That is not true as landlords are required to provide them, regardless if they have ever personally occupied the property or not.

Please note, if a seller does not provide a seller disclosure statement and is legally required to do so, then the buyer most likely has a legal right to terminate the deal all the way up until closing and have their earnest money deposit refunded. Important to note, the seller disclosure statement is usually not part of the purchase and sale agreement. It is a form that Washington State law requires most residential property sellers to fill out and provide to a buyer. There is no due date or rule that a seller should have this filled out when they list. I always advise sellers that I work with to complete this seller disclosure statement prior to the listing going live and answer every question truthfully and to their best ability. If a buyer or seller has content related questions about this form, they need to consult with a local real estate attorney for help. A real estate agent is not allowed to provide help with answering or interpreting the contents/answers on this form. The seller's agent can check to make sure the most current version of this form has been provided and all applicable questions are answered, explanations provided if required, and all pages are properly signed/initialed by the seller. That's it; anything else requires assistance from a real estate attorney. One thing I do caution a seller when completing the seller disclosure statement is answering *"don't know"* to every question or the majority of questions. That is not going to help you out should problems arise. If you have knowledge about defects in your property, you are legally required to disclose them, as is your agent should she learn of any material facts or defects with your property. Consult with a local real estate attorney for help but unless you truly do not know something, do not just blindly check off the *"don't know"* box.

It is important to also keep in mind, while your house is listed if a new material fact about your house or property is discovered then legally you need to amend/update your seller disclosure statement. This is especially true if you have a buyer who does an inspection and it reveals several new material defects that you are now aware of. This buyer backs out of the deal. Legally you need to fill out a new seller disclosure form and include the new material defects/facts that you now know as a result of the previous buyer's inspection. At any point, if your agent becomes aware of any material fact regarding your property she is legally required to inform any potential buyer of this fact and should advise that you also inform prospective buyers/the public via your seller disclosure form. Do not try to hide any new fact that you learn of during the selling process. I can almost guarantee you that it will come back to haunt you.

HOME SELLING FOR SMARTIES

A great deal of lawsuits against sellers occurs as a result of them not revealing known facts to the buyer. An example of this would be a seller who knows their septic tank is defective. They make no mention of this fact to their listing agent and do not disclose it on their seller disclosure form. The buyer's inspection does not reveal this condition. The deal closes and three months later the septic system fails, the buyer hires a repair company to come out. While repairing it the next door neighbor tells the new owner that you (the previous owner) knew there was a bad septic tank in the ground and had been hoping for the best for years. That's the start of the lawsuit against you. Neighbors always talk once you have moved out, so make your life a lot easier and reveal all known material facts and defects that you know about your property ahead of time!

This does not sound difficult does it? I could rant for pages as to how frustrating the seller disclosure form can be when I am a buyer's agent. Please keep in mind, that the seller disclosure statement is not a guarantee for the buyer that they then know all the problems/issues a property may have. It is merely a jumping off point and if you have any questions or doubts as to what you should or should not reveal to a buyer via this form or otherwise, you should always consult with a local real estate attorney before proceeding.

Legal Description...

The final piece of paper you should acknowledge when listing your property (in WA State) is the legal description. Some states have rules that require this description be directly entered into the purchase and sale agreement, while others do not require a legal description at all

89

in order to reach mutual agreement. The legal description is usually a short paragraph provided by the title company which describes the property, "*Baylor Division, subplot two, lot six, block three of parcel seven-A of the Atkins Addition, etc....*" a real stimulating read! In Washington State, in order for an offer to technically be mutually agreed upon, the legal description must be acknowledged (initialed) by both the seller and the buyer. A good listing agent will have ordered preliminary title when she takes a listing and the title company will provide her with the legal description for the property. She will have you initial and date it and hopefully post the legal description with her listing on the MLS when the listing goes live. Dating items that you initial or sign is not always legally necessary, but a good agent is going to insist that you date everything for clarity. There have been incidents where the seller did not provide a legal description and/or only one side acknowledged it. This technically leaves a legal gap and one could argue that failure to obtain a mutually acknowledged legal description means mutual acceptance did not occur. Obviously, to make things more user friendly for a buyer and their agent and to help facilitate an offer on your property, the legal description should be available online with your listing and ready to go. It is very important that the legal description be mutually signed around with the offer forms. If you live in another state, check to see what the rules are there regarding the legal description.

Insurance and Valuables...

Prior to listing your home for sale and going live, your agent should have you contact your current home insurance provider. You should let them know you are listing your house for sale and ask if there is any additional coverage that you as a home owner should have while your home is on the market. You want to know what happens if a buyer is touring and falls and breaks their leg in your house? What happens if a buyer breaks your Ming Dynasty vase? What if the buyer's agent forgets to shut and lock the front door and your house is robbed? See what they tell you and act accordingly. This is a good place to mention what I always tell my sellers. Prior to listing, you want to remove all irreplaceable valuables from your property. The Ming Dynasty vase, your grandma's quilt, your jewelry, whatever it is, take it out and store it somewhere off-site that is safe. As previously mentioned, also remove and replace any real property items like the chandelier or front door knocker that you intend to take with you. Go through your medicine cabinet and remove all prescription drugs. I have clients who store their prescription drugs in the trunk of their car while their house is on the market. There are endless stories of seller's prescription drugs being stolen at open houses or while a buyer is touring. Take them out. Do not leave your checkbook, bank statements, bills, credit cards, or cash lying around. Just imagine that your house is now a department store and you are going to have buyers wandering through your home, just like a department store does. You want to mitigate lose and take measures to make sure items are not stolen.

Pets...

If you have pets, you need to plan in advance what you are going to do with them while your house is listed for sale. Everyone thinks their dog is friendly and that may be true in your case. However, if you have a dog (no matter how small) it is going to be best if you can remove her during showings of your property. Many buyers and agents are afraid of dogs, big or small. Putting your dog in a kennel in the backyard or in your home is not really the best option either. The dog is typically not happy with that situation and becomes scared or angry when strangers show up and tromp through his den. Even if your pooch is caged, some buyers who are touring could still be afraid of the dog and even though your dog is secured, the buyers may subconsciously hurry out of your house or not linger, because they are scared of the dog. So when possible, remove any size dog from your property for all showings.

Then there are our feline friends. The main concern with cats in the house while showing is them escaping. I have blocked many a cat trying to escape out the front door when I am unlocking it to show buyers. This adds a diversion to the showing and it is best if potential buyers can focus exclusively on your property not your cats. This also creeps up if the agent or buyers are cat lovers and your friendly cat follows them around while touring. As a huge animal lover myself, I can tell you if your home has a friendly cat there while I am showing buyers, I am going to get distracted and pet and play with the cat, guaranteed. Some cat owners, who have cats that like to escape, will confine their cat to one room. The room's door is closed with a warning sign on it. This can work if there is no alternative. The main thing is that you are fully aware that any pet you leave in your home when an agent is showing, there is a risk he will escape. Some agents are completely out to lunch when showing a house and do not notice the sign on the front door warning them not to let the cat out. You need to realize even a diligent agent might accidently let your cat out or your pet may outsmart them and make a break for it.

Other pets such as hamsters, rabbits, and snakes are usually confined to a cage so there is not as much of an issue. That said, many years ago I was showing a house to buyers. There was no notation in the agent listing report as to any pets in the house and no signs posted anywhere in the house indicating there were pets. One door in the basement rec. room was closed and my buyer opened it and commented on how there appeared to be an extra room. She fumbled around and found the light switch. She also found a huge python quickly unraveling in the corner who was not pleased to have been so rudely awakened! We got out of there in record time. The listing agent should have noted this in the listing report and put a sign on the door. The seller should not have left that snake loose in the room even if signs were posted. In another case a couple of years ago, I unlocked the front door for buyers at a house where we had made an appointment to tour it in advance. Nothing indicated there were any pets inside. What did we encounter? A very aggressive and angry pit bull that lunged at us and practically tore the front door down once I managed to get us outside and the door shut. What were the first words out of my buyers' mouths? *"We could have sued them if that dog hurt us."* So take heed from the buying public, you need an agent to help you plan for and handle your pets in advance. You as a seller should never leave yourself open to a lawsuit by leaving a pit bull or python unattended when your house is being shown.

Extra Steps For a Condo...

A condominium sale has a few extra steps that a single family home sale does not have. With a condo you will be requesting and receiving a Resale Certificate and the CC&Rs. This will be indicated on the first page of the condominium purchase and sale agreement (in WA State). The seller pays for the Resale Certificate and the accompanying documents, the CC&Rs (covenants, conditions, and regulations). This typically includes all rules, regulations, and bylaws for the condo, board meeting minutes, financial and reserve account information (something the buyer's loan person is going to want a copy of), any current litigation against the home owner's association, any special assessments, anticipated repairs, the current owner occupancy ratio, and types of financing the complex is approved for. If there are any pending lawsuits against the association then the buyer's loan person most likely will not be able to lend money to the buyer to purchase until the suit is settled.

The seller has to order the Resale Certificate and the CC&Rs from the management company that manages the condo complex. This usually costs anywhere between $300 and $500. It can take the management company 10 days, sometimes even longer to provide these documents. This step usually drives the seller and their agent crazy. Condo management companies unfortunately do not typically have a user friendly reputation for this process! If your condo complex is self managed, then a MLS Resale Certificate form should be

94

provided to the appointed person who fills out those documents for the self managed complex. Your agent should forward that document and the CC&Rs to the buyer's agent as soon as it is delivered and you have reviewed and signed off as the seller. The buyer's agent will send all the documents to the buyer who then has to sign it. In Washington State, the buyer then has five days to review a Resale Certificate and CC&Rs. Your agent should get a copy of the buyer's signature for receipt of these documents from the buyer's agent and she should also check in with the buyer's lender to make sure the buyer's agent has forwarded them a complete copy of the Resale Certificate. The buyer's lender is going to need a copy of the completed, signed around Resale Certificate in order for them to go forward with the buyer's loan. There could unfortunately be a condition noted in the Resale that disqualifies the buyer's lender from lending the buyer money to purchase your unit. If that is the case, your deal is dead.

During the Resale Certificate review period, the buyer can ask any questions that may come up, verify that the condo's rules are okay with them. You the seller should not be directly answering any questions pertaining to the management or rules and regulations of the condo complex. The buyer needs to be getting answers to their questions regarding the condo complex directly from the condo management company and/or the home owner association contact person. If for some reason there is a rule or condition that a buyer cannot live with, they can terminate the transaction based on the Resale Certificate and CC&Rs review. If their agent keeps them within the review deadline time period and files the paperwork properly then the buyer's earnest money deposit should be refundable.

As a seller you need to be prepared ahead of time for how annoying this part of the process can be. You can spend $500 for a Resale Certificate only to have the buyer terminate the deal based on their review of the Resale. Unfortunately, you will most likely have to order and pay for a new Resale Certificate when a new buyer and offer comes along. Legally, it is not wise to reuse a pre-existing Resale Certificate or the CC&Rs. I advise my condo sellers to first contact their condo management company before listing to find out exactly what these documents will cost and what the turn-around time period is from the day you order them to the day you will receive them. We need to know that time frame in advance before you sign off on an offer and agree to a delivery timeline for these documents. You also need to find out if they provide these documents in hard copy format, as there are still many buyers who prefer and will request, via their offer, that you provide these documents in hard copy not just a PDF version. You should also consult with a local real estate attorney to find out what, if any, parts of these documents you could possibly reuse if you pay for these documents and the deal goes south.

Sometimes a seller orders the Resale Certificate and CC&Rs when they first list their condo so they are readily available when a buyer's offer is accepted. Legally you should find out how long these documents are valid; i.e. they might expire before you get an offer. Also, certain lenders will only accept a new and up-to-date version of these documents and will not fund the buyer's loan without them or portions of them.

You can see providing these documents is expensive and takes time. Why they are so expensive is in my opinion not justifiable. In my opinion, it is merely a way for the condo management company to hold a seller hostage and earn big bucks for documents only they can provide. Pulling these items up and printing or sending them over as a PDF does not take that much time or in my opinion legitimizes such a high fee. The Resale Certificate is usually a few pages, where the appropriate management company official fills in standard blanks. The sometimes voluminous CC&Rs are almost all boilerplate. Seems like an online access system could be implemented by the condo management companies, where the CC&R boilerplate is posted and accessible for any prospective buyer/lender to review and the latest board meeting minutes, and financial statements are accessible via a password. A hard copy Resale Certificate would probably still need to be provided but the bulk of the documents could be handled online via password access. How providing these documents to condo owners warrants the management company charging so much is beyond me!

I will caution you as a condo seller, do not be tempted to keep these documents on file and alter them in any way should your first deal go south and you want to reuse these documents for your next deal. It is tempting, but altering these documents can be illegal. Please avoid the listing agent who says they will provide you with "free" copies of the condos CC&Rs if you list with them. You have no way of knowing where the documents came from and when they were printed. You could potentially get in a world of trouble later on if it was determined that you provided a buyer with out of date or altered Resale/CC&R documents. If you are still wondering about reusing any portion of the Resale Certificate and/or CC&Rs, then your agent should instruct you to consult with a local real estate attorney and have them advise you in writing as to what is best to do.

I think the Resale Certificate and CC&Rs review process for a condo is a bit backwards but this is how it is currently handled in Washington State.

Here is a **tip**, your agent should always make sure you review and sign the Resale Certificate before it is delivered to the buyer's agent. The buyer then needs to sign and date the Resale upon receipt and his five day review period (in WA State) then begins. Your agent should make sure the buyer's agent sends over a copy of the buyer's signed receipt of the Resale Certificate. Many years ago, I had a buyer purchasing a condominium. When we got the Resale Certificate, the listing agent had not gotten her seller to sign it where required. I contacted the listing agent and asked her to get the seller to sign it. Despite my numerous reminders, the listing agent never got her seller to sign the Resale. So, about a week before the scheduled closing date my buyer up and decides he no longer wanted to go through with the purchase of the condominium. He had already waived his inspection and financing contingencies. However, the seller never signed the Resale Certificate and that is what we used to get him out of the deal and his earnest money deposit refunded. Had the seller signed the Resale Certificate where required and before delivery to the buyer, my client would not have had a legal way to terminate his deal at the last minute and at a minimum he would have lost his earnest money deposit. Do not let this happen to you as a seller. Hire someone who is detail oriented and knows how to keep you out of these kinds of situations!

Another **tip** for a condo listing is to make sure your listing agent is properly filling out the condominium listing report. If your unit comes with a parking space and a storage unit, your agent should be noting in the listing report the location and number of the parking space and the storage unit. Once your property is listed, hopefully your agent is going to forward you a copy of the MLS Agent Detail Report and Client Detail Report. These sheets show you exactly what a buyer's agent is going to pull up and review regarding your listing and what they will be giving to their client to review. In the Agent Detail Report for your condominium listing are blanks to indicate the parking space number and storage unit number. Without fail, every time I have condo buyers at least half of these reports do not mention there is a parking space or storage unit, when in fact there are! That definitely costs you the condo seller time and money. Parking spaces and storage units in condo world are gold! Some reports might indicate that there is one parking space or a storage unit, but provide no information as to where they are located. Most buyers want to see the parking space and storage unit when they are touring.

A while back I had a condo buyer and the listing report for a vacant condo we were touring indicated there was one parking space included but did not provide a space number or location. My buyer wanted to see the parking space to make sure her car would fit in it. I called the listing agent but got voice mail. Two days later after I left a voice mail and sent an email asking about the parking space number/location the listing agent responded. She said she didn't know where it was located and to ask the condo management company. I then asked her who the management company was as her listing report did not provide that information; those blanks were not filled in either! I was amazed she actually knew who the management company was.

I called the condo management company and they told me the seller needed to give them permission in writing first before they could provide me the unit's parking space number. I relayed that information back to the listing agent several times but never heard back from her. My buyer was ticked off and decided she didn't want to consider living in a condo complex that was this difficult. So she purchased another condo in a different complex. Three weeks or so later, I got a call from the original condo seller. She said she had run into the condo manager while checking her vacant unit and he let her know that I had a buyer who wanted to know her unit's parking space number. I relayed the story above and let her know my buyer had moved on. She was not thrilled. Nor should she have been. However, the seller should not have hired a listing agent to represent her who did not complete important information on the listing report and who could not be bothered to respond or help prospective buyers with information they wanted.

1031 Exchange...

One final thing to consider if applicable, when you sell your property, if it is an investment property then you may want to consider doing a 1031 exchange. This is something your agent needs to note in your listing report that is posted on the MLS and buyers need to know about this in advance. It usually does not affect a buyer but it still should be noted in the purchase and sale agreement paperwork so all terms are fully disclosed. A 1031 exchange allows an investor to postpone paying income tax on any gains in the sale of the investment property if the proceeds are reinvested in a similar property. Usually your personal residence does not qualify. If you think this may apply to your situation, your agent should put you in touch with a 1031 exchange facilitator and you should also consult with your tax person for more detailed and specific information.

Real Life...

Many years ago, I took out a client on a tour to see some high end properties. The fourth house we were scheduled to see on our tour was an old estate in a very expensive and exclusive neighborhood. It had struck us both as very odd that this grand house only had exterior photographs posted and not a word was said about the interior besides the number of bedrooms and baths and that the buyer should bring their imagination and could upgrade this historic home to their liking. That immediately had me thinking the interior must be very dated and perhaps not in the best condition. However, the exterior shots showed the house to be well cared for and maintained. The pool out back was sparkling in the online photo. I made an appointment as

101

required with the listing agent and she warned me that the inside might be a bit tricky but to have my buyer focus on the "bones" of the house, the potential and remind her of the exclusive neighborhood this house was in. As an afterthought, she told me not to worry about letting the cats out as they were free to come and go as they pleased. I warned the buyer we might be seeing a house that was a bit shoddy inside. Boy, were we surprised.

Shoddy did not begin to describe the stinking, hoarder's nest we found! When I opened the front door the first thing that hit us was the stench of cat urine, beyond what you would smell at a cat rescue center. Cat urine was embedded in the house's hardwood flooring and there must have been at least sixty or more cats living in this enormous house. The entry's marble floors were clean and did have a nice table with flyers on it but from there it was unreal. There were cats and feces and cat food everywhere. The kitchen was almost completely covered in hoarding crap and assorted cats were everywhere. The living room and study were nice and not filled with junk. However, the cats had shredded all of the custom drapery, the high end chintz sofas, all the Aubusson rugs were completely destroyed by cat excrement. We found our way upstairs, trying not to let the stench make us ill. We were in the master bedroom when my client let out a gasp, there was someone in the bed and they were not awake. No one was supposed to be in the house. We quickly hurried out and I called the listing agent. She told me that the seller was probably in bed again. She apparently had a sleeping pill addiction and this had happened before. Since we did not wake the owner up when we were in the room, I thought it best to have an ambulance come out just to make sure. Thankfully, it was not a dead owner in the bed but the ER people did take her away to the hospital I guess to pump her stomach, and revive her.

The client was not amused or impressed. Talk about a creepy experience. What this house was doing on the market is anyone's guess. I don't know why the listing agent had even bothered. This is an extreme example, but hopefully it shows that what I have said about prepping your property before listing really is a wise idea.

FIVE

GOING LIVE

You have now taken care of the seemingly endless prep work and it is time for your property listing to go live! Preparing your house as outlined in this book probably has not been a walk in the park, but you now know that you have done the very best you can to make your property show well and be buyer friendly. Going live, and having your property listed is still no picnic either but at least your prep work should help you in terms of selling your house as fast as possible.

Listing Details...

Your real estate agent should have shown you the listing paperwork and you should have reviewed and approved by signing, the marketing verbiage and information about your house that is going to appear on the MLS. Your house will be assigned an MLS number and agents and buyers will be viewing your property online. They will see the photographs of your house (hopefully good as discussed) and they will see the pertinent information; how many bedrooms and baths, the square footage, annual taxes, etc.... They also will read the fluff (marketing remarks) your agent will write to entice buyers to stop by your house and take a look. Hopefully it is not too noxious, as some real estate agent prose is completely over the top; in fact I keep a file of humorous ones I come across. Unfortunately, when it comes to listing verbiage, stupid is not in short supply! For example one agent posted this for his client's house. Personally, I cannot understand why the seller even remotely thought this was cute or would help to sell the property. But hey, this agent and seller clearly agreed on hokey, Hello Kitty prose, something for everyone! To describe this house, the agent entered the following on the MLS and on the marketing flyers, *"I'm a cute lost kitty looking for a good owner to adopt me! I'm a bit scruffy and need some grooming but I have a sweet heart and good bones! A bit of TLC and I'll use my litter box and purr for you! I can be your kitty for the right price, meow!!!"*

Then there is this convoluted prose from a high end listing, *"The ingenuity of mélange with pigments of Spain, lush sienna and mustard yellow with a soft burgundy coating gleeful surfaces of plaster walls. International assemblages of cultural artwork harmonizing to ease and enrich the diversity. The enthusiastic décor awash in a patina of textures. Romance is shimmering in this abode on stage from dawn to dusk. Détente!"* We won't even bother to try and decipher exactly what this listing agent was attempting to convey. At a minimum, there is the improper grammar, the lack of any substantive facts about the property. The seller should have given the agent a dictionary and forbidden the use of foreign words. How a seller could be selling a high end property and allow that kind of nonsensical drivel to describe their house to prospective buyers is beyond me. If your agent cannot compose listing verbiage that makes sense and is grammatically correct, then what else are they incapable of handling; i.e. offer negotiations, legal notices, forms, transaction deadlines, etc...?

I kid you not this kind of listing verbiage bunk is everywhere! I think far too many agents have been to clock hour classes on "telling a story" via the listing verbiage. Some of these stories, in my opinion, are better left unsaid as they do not do you the seller any favors. At a minimum, idiotic marketing verbiage makes the agent looks like a complete fool but it also lets the buyer know the seller is either equally grammatically challenged or not very smart. In my opinion, less is more and the use of foreign words is not impressive, even if they are used correctly.

Once you have approved the listing verbiage, you and your agent need to discuss access to your house. Most listings now have key boxes installed and hopefully they are properly secured to something more substantive than a small shrub's branch. User friendly access does work to your advantage but this does not mean you cannot set some parameters for showings. Many people like to have their home shown while they are away at work, or no showings after 7:00 p.m. or before 11:00 a.m. What works best for your property? Do keep in mind, the easier access an agent has to show your property, the more showings you are likely to have.

You still need to be prepared for the rude and/or clueless agent that literally barges in on you and tries to show. For example, I had a listing a while back and my client wanted 24 hours notice for all showings and did not want her place shown before 10:00 a.m. This was clearly stated in her property's listing report; any buyer's agent who can read knew what the seller wanted and what the showing instructions were. Just in case, I also, posted a laminated sign on her front door in bold lettering, reminding agents they needed to provide 24 hour advance notice prior to showing, per the listing report. Naturally, 8:30 a.m. on a Sunday, who should start banging on the seller's door, while unlocking it and waking her up? A pushy agent with her client in tow, "*Oh, did I wake you? Well, we just want to take a quick peek at your place. We won't be too long. We are on a tight tour schedule today. You know you really need to let us in, you don't want to miss out on a potential sale now do you?*" Fortunately, my seller refused to allow her to come in even though this rude agent persisted in trying to weasel her way inside. My seller let me know about this incident and I looked up the agent's information on the electronic key box report and called the agent's designated broker and reported her to the local MLS for violating showing rules. In my opinion, there is no excuse for this at all. Any buyer's agent that cannot plan a client tour in advance, read and follow the posted showing instructions (in the listing report and in this case on a sign right there on the front door), should not be selling real estate. As my Home Buying For Smarties book states in this example, hopefully the buyer fired this agent and found someone better to represent them. Unfortunately far too many people think a real estate agent's license is a license to be rude and nosy (they might benefit from my forthcoming agent training book).

Once you have your key box and showing rules set, make sure you remember that all agents who enter your property are required by law to leave their business card. Usually a seller will set up an area in the house with flyers and or maybe a dish of candy/flowers and a spot for all agents to leave their business cards. If someone enters your property and fails to leave their business card, I hope your agent reports them, as there is no excuse for this.

Letters and Forms on File...

One last detail to take care of before your listing is live is to first make sure your agent is posting the title company and preliminary title order number online with your listing , the legal description (if required in your state), and the seller disclosure statement. Also, if your home was built prior to 1978 you are required by the government to provide a Lead Disclosure Form 22-J (in WA State). This form must be signed by you, your agent, the buyer and the buyer's agent and you indicate if you know of any lead paint issues with your property. The buyer then has to sign such that they acknowledge the risk of lead paint in your home and they can also conduct a lead paint assessment test if they wish. For what it is worth, I have never had a buyer do a lead paint assessment test. We know if the house is 1978 or older then there is lead paint somewhere and so do not eat or sniff, any chipping paint to avoid lead exposure. Anyway, you should have your agent post this form with your listing if your home was built prior to 1978.

In addition to these basic forms and information that should go with your listing, your agent should also be posting any letters on file that are required. This would be a letter where you acknowledge that you are only interested in seeing any offers on a specific date; this your agent may suggest doing if you are trying to create a multiple offer scenario. Your agent should also post if you have any specific showing limitations or only want to see offers from buyers that include a pre-approval loan letter, etc.... It is real easy to get this information taken care of ahead of time and posted with your listing per the MLS rules. It amazes me how many listing agents do not do this, and later on troubles and disputes arise, big surprise. Make sure your agent is doing this is my strong advice.

Open House...

Your agent and you should have discussed how you are going to handle any broker's opens or public open houses. A broker's open is the traditional way agents used to publicize and spread the word about your listing. They were especially important back in the day when listings were published in the books. To get the word out about your listing to other agents, your agent would hold a broker's open. These are opens that are for licensed agents only and usually occur on a weekday for a couple of hours. Some listing agents still do these but many have stopped. Attendance at broker's opens has plummeted as this business has moved online, electronic key boxes are now the common way to gain access to a listing (as opposed to the old way of picking up keys at the local listing office) and agents are less specialized in specific areas or neighborhoods. All of this has combined to make the broker's open almost passé in some places. I know when I hold a broker's open these days, attendance is way down and in some cases non-existent. I prepare my sellers for this low turnout in advance.

Along these lines here is a **tip,** there are some agents who hoard other real estate agents business cards and then when they hold a broker's open or a public open house they put this cache of cards out so the seller is impressed with how many agents they think have been through their property. Another common trick is they will collect business cards from the other brokers in their office and then put that stack out at their broker's open and brag about how active and supportive their brokerage/agents are with listings. Total fraud but many sellers just eat it right up! This was more common years ago but it still happens today. I have always found it stupid as well as deceptive.

Besides the brokers opens there are open houses. Open houses are traditionally times set aside when the general public has access to tour your house. This would be when your nosey neighbors free range through your place and comment non-stop on your taste in furniture, décor, etc.... These used to be published once a week in the Sunday newspaper and the hoards would attend. This too has dramatically fallen off since this industry has moved online. In fact, who do you know who still gets and reads the hard copy of their local Sunday newspaper? I used to be a Sunday open house fanatic. If I did not have a listing to promote, then I would always sit another agent's listing for them on Sunday. I enjoyed them. I kept very detailed records for each open house I did, charting the number of people through and how they learned about the open house. I noticed around 2005 things really turned. It became rare that anyone was saying they learned about the open house from the newspaper and attendance continued to drop. Also, most people attending were already working with a buyer's agent and in many cases their buyer's agent was there with them. It started to make less sense to hold open houses as most of the public was moving to having a buyer's agent represent them from the start and thus arrange all of their house tours. You can learn more about this topic in my Home Buying For Smarties book.

Another big change that occurred with public open houses is the issue of safety. I always advise agents to hold an open house with another agent or a mortgage broker. This way they have company but more important there is safety in numbers and more eyes to monitor who is coming through and what they are doing. Unfortunately, many would-be burglars attend open houses and scope out the goods and how to best access the place. Some learn through the clueless agent holding the open house that the sellers are currently out of town but expected back next Wednesday. This has been a growing problem and concern and many home owners no longer want their agent to hold open houses for their property.

You and your agent should have discussed the pros and cons of brokers opens and public open houses and decided yea or nay if you are going to do them with your listing or not.

Living in a Magazine Spread...

While your house is listed for sale it really is akin to living in a magazine spread or you feel like a fish in bowl, all open and exposed to the world. It's not fun but you need to try and cope with it as best you can. As mentioned, your listing agent has probably given you a checklist of fire drill items you need to attend to before any showings or before you take off to work each day. It gets old very fast but it is in your best interest. I have had clients who have actually decided after their place has been on the market a bit, to literally move out and stay with a friend or rent a short stay hotel suite for the remainder of time their place is on the market. This may be something you want to consider. This will make showings a lot easier for buyer agents,

111

because if your house is then "vacant" or can be shown pretty much any time of the day or night while the key box access is activated and you might get more showings. You'll still want to check in on your house from time to time, pick up your mail, check to make sure lights are on that should be, plants are watered, things are still show ready. But not living on the premises makes your daily fire drill a lot less challenging. This is not always an option but something to ponder if living in the magazine spread starts to become too challenging.

Flyers...

Marketing flyers are the traditional way listing agents promoted your property. Today, there are email marketing blasts, a zillion websites your listing will be posted on besides the MLS and there are QR codes. Far fewer listings have marketing flyer boxes posted on the yard sign anymore, and probably for good reason. Those flyer boxes were always getting vandalized, the flyers stolen, the rain soaking them, on and on. Most people who are interested in your property are now going to learn about if first online, or they are going to call your agent listed on the sign for more information, or call their buyer's agent and have them get more information. In my opinion, the flyers posted outside are really a waste of paper and a pain for the seller and listing agent to keep on top of. Some agents now will post one flyer inside the listing, highlighting the house's features or they may still leave a pile of them for people who are touring to pick up. Most informed buyers are going to be working with a buyer's agent who provides them with client print out reports (from the MLS) for each property they are touring. The buyers usually make their notes on each property on the tour sheets. Some will pick up a listing's marketing flyer off the kitchen's counter when touring but I have noticed this too is way less now that we are in a digital world. Even though the hard copy marketing flyers appear to be dying off, I still carry a stack of them with me each day when I am out and about and give them to anyone I think might be interested in my client's listing.

Showings...

After all of your hard work prepping the place, the first showings that you have will be exciting for you. Unfortunately, the novelty of that wears off after the first three or so showings and then it is just an automatic fire drill routine. If your agent has secured a key box outside your house then you do not have to worry about leaving it outside and putting it back in doors. Your agent should have tested the key copies you made for your house prior to placing them in the key box to ensure they actually unlock the doors. Remember, you want to make it as easy as possible for a buyer's agent to enter your home! Sometimes it makes good sense to go ahead and rekey your locks prior to listing and have say your doorknob lock and the deadbolt keyed for one key. This keeps things very simple and easy and that's one less key a ditzy buyer's agent can lose when showing your home. You also want to make sure there are lights left on or automatic timers so the agent can see to access the key box outside and when the buyer walks into the front door your house is not completely dark and uninviting. For a vacant property this is especially important. Also, make sure the heat is left on a comfortable setting or the air conditioning if you are in warmer climes. Again, this is really important if your property is vacant. It is almost expected now that agents and buyers will remove their shoes when touring your home. Still your agent might want to hang up a sign indicating that request. Your agent might also leave a basket of those blue Smurf shoe covers as well; the type of shoe covers they use in the hospital operating rooms. Those however, are really cumbersome and most buyers now opt to just take off their shoes.

Regardless of what your showing rules and hours are going to be, it is important that you vacate your house while it is being shown. Potential buyers and their agents need to be able to look at your place and speak freely. If you are hovering around it really hinders things. If you are really insistent, then at the very least you should stand outside on the front door step or lawn and wait until they are done. This still adds pressure to the buyers while touring your property and is not something I recommend you do. It is best if you leave, are not there when any buyers arrive. You can go for a walk, maybe walk your dog while the place is being shown. You can request that the buyer's agent call your cell phone to let you know when they through showing and have locked everything back up. Lingering around your house while it is being shown is really not in your best interest. They need to be able to take everything in on their own, unhindered, and see things for themselves. There is nothing worse than when a seller lingers and starts asking, *"Did you notice the new hot tub out back and did your agent tell you that the tile flooring is new and what other properties are you all looking at?"* Get out and let the buyers and their agent have some breathing room and notice what is important to them. I can understand "hovering sellers" on some level, you want to make sure your nest is okay and you want to make sure everyone appreciates it for the great place it is, but it is in your best interest to stay away while it is being shown. When I am working as a buyer's agent and we encounter a seller who hovers, I can assure you that it bothers the buyers and they really are less inclined to fully take in your house and make an offer on your place.

Once someone has toured your home, if your key box is the electronic kind, your listing agent should receive a message that provides the showing agent's name and the time they accessed the key box. A good listing agent is going to contact them for feedback. She will ask if the agent was previewing or actually showing your place to buyers. Then there are the standard questions you may want to have your agent ask. These include what they thought of the property in comparison to others that are listed, what they think about the list price, any suggestions, etc.... Your agent will most likely email the showing agent and hopefully include a photo of your property, the address, and MLS number in the feedback request. When I am working with buyers, I can sometimes see 50 or more properties in a week and they all blur in my mind. When I receive a feedback request from a listing agent that does not include a photo of the property and the address, do you think I am going to take the time to try and figure out which listing this was? Not likely, so no feedback. Hopefully your agent is aware of this and knows how to make their feedback request user-friendly. It's not that difficult but at least half of the feedback requests I get overlook the obvious! Also, hopefully your listing agent is not calling the showing agent for feedback. A busy buyer's agent does not have time to talk to every listing agent calling for feedback, it's annoying. And it is stupid. Again, what buyer's agent can recall off the top of their head Suzie Listing Agent's listing in Colonial Park, especially if they showed a few houses in that area. Also, even if your agent sends a user friendly feedback request via email, quite a lot of buyer's agents will not bother responding so be prepared for this lack of feedback.

While your listing agent might ask for feedback on the list price, only a naïve or careless buyer's agent is going to provide that information to them. A good buyer's agent will never provide an answer for this price question. Why is that? This story will explain.

I was a listing agent a few years back for a house and I sent out my feedback email on the property to an agent that had just shown it, letting her know my sellers had requested and appreciated any feedback on the property. She responded back with detailed answers. She said her buyer was very interested in the house and regarding the list price question, stated the buyer and she both thought it was priced right. I relayed this feedback to my sellers as required by law. A day later the buyer's agent submitted an offer. They offered less than the list price, although via the latest active/sold comps the list price was of fair market value. My seller countered back at full price. The seller cited the agent/buyer's feedback from the previous day, i.e. that the list price was accurate. What more could the buyer or their agent say? The comps showed the list price was good and they themselves said it was an accurate price. Game over! My sellers got full list price. Thus, a smart buyer's agent is not going to provide your agent with any pricing feedback as it may not be in his buyer's best interest to do so.

One final point I want to mention with showings, is the condition that is sometimes placed that the listing agent must be present for all showings. This is really unnecessary in my opinion. Today, all buyers' agents are tracked via the electronic key boxes and they are required by law to leave their business card when showing. Having your listing agent at your house when a buyer is shown the property does not help sell your place and does not add any real protection or security for your house. Usually, the listing agent that is required to be there opens the door for the buyer and their agent, says hello and then sits outside or in the kitchen and does work on their laptop while the house is shown.

A buyer does not want your agent following along behind him and his agent and listening in on their comments or reading their reaction. It's annoying. Many upper end agents will agree to be present for showings, in order to puff up their seller's egos; i.e. *my house is so grand that I require my agent be present for all showings.* In some rare cases, this kind of requirement might be warranted but the vast majority of listings that require this is as a showing condition, do not warrant it.

This type of showing restriction can also greatly reduce the number of showings your property gets. The buyer's agent now has to coordinate her schedule, the buyer's schedule as well as your listing agent's schedule and availability. Plus, it has to work with the flow of the buyer's tour; i.e. coordinating with the other properties they are looking at that day. I would not advise you request this as a condition to listing your property.

117

The worst are the condominium boards that require this as a stipulation for all listings in their building. These poor condo listing agents usually show up and wait in the hall while the unit is shown. I suspect a good many of the condominiums that have this kind of out-dated showing regulation, originally had this restriction written in by an agent who lived in the building and wanted to try and secure all of the listings in the complex where they lived. What a better way to beat out a competing agent for a listing than to be able to tell a prospective seller, *"I live in this building so I am readily available at any time to be present for any showings."* Again, this type of restriction usually means your pool of viable prospective buyers is reduced. Many times, I have had buyers tell me that they want to forget touring a certain listing because it has this kind of showing restriction and the listing agent is unable to accommodate the buyer's tour date and time.

Upkeep...

If you want your property to sell as quickly as possible and you want to get top dollar, it is crucial that you keep your place looking as good as possible at all times, even after you have an offer. This means making sure the yard is well maintained, if you have a patio or balcony keep it clean and fresh plants/flowers in pots at all times. It is tempting once your place has been listed for a while or once you have a signed around deal to slack off but that will only hurt you. It's a major pain but worth your time and effort in the end. Do not go to all this trouble prepping your property to make it all show pony ready and then once your deal is signed around turn your place into a pigsty.

Your property still needs to look great for the inspection, appraisal, buyer's final walk through, closing day.

Real Life...

A while back I had a buyer I was working with and she was in the market for a single family home in an upscale suburban area. I set up her tour and the third house on the tour required 24 hour advance notice. The listing report said to contact the seller's phone to show number and if no one was there to leave a message stating the date and time you intended to show. If you called ahead by 24 hours and did not hear back then assume all was good and go show. This is exactly what I did, I left a message in advance letting the seller know we would be there on Saturday between 3 and 4 p.m. and I left my number in case this did not work or the seller needed to cancel at the last minute. We arrived around 3:15 and I noticed a number of cars parked on the street out front as well as a few in the drive way. I assumed the sellers might be home and have guests. I warned my buyer that we might have to work our tour around some kind of function the seller appeared to be having. Since it was cold outside I doubted whatever function they might be having would be outside in the back yard. I rang the front doorbell but did not hear it. I assumed it was broken (something you should fix prior to listing your home). I knocked on the front door and called out when I unlocked and opened it. Dead silence. Well maybe the seller had friends who parked their cars at the house and then they all went off somewhere else? My buyer and I started looking around. The house was spotless; we toured the main level, went upstairs and checked out the four bedrooms there. In the kitchen I looked out the glass doors but saw the grassy back yard was empty. My buyer was taking her notes and we decided to check out the basement level before we left. According to the listing report, it boasted two full family rooms and another bed and bath. The basement was dark and the lighting was low. The first room appeared to be a TV room with a pool table and there were some clothes and cocktail glasses scattered around but nothing too unusual. The stereo was on fairly loud playing techno synthesizer music. We heard some muffled sounds coming from the next room. We went down a narrow hallway passing a small laundry room and the muffled sounds grew louder. I called out again asking if anyone was home, etc... By this time my buyer had entered the dark room at the end of the hall and she quickly turned around and motioned for me to leave. Apparently we had walked in on an orgy the sellers were hosting.

We were both pretty shocked and quickly hot footed it back upstairs and out the front door. No one ever emerged or yelled out after us, so I do not think they even had a clue that we were there, had been there. I called the listing agent and let her know we had made an appointment, followed the showing instructions and let her know what we had walked in on. She was completely unsurprised, *"Oh the sellers are at it again, hosting another one of their nude parties huh? I'm sure you gave your showing notice but the sellers often forget to check their voice mail. Let me know if your buyer has any interest in making an offer, I know my sellers are very interested in moving on to a warmer weather state."* Yeah, so they can have their nude parties outside?

HOME SELLING FOR SMARTIES

So, just in case you regularly host orgies at your house or whatever, please make sure you do check your voice mail frequently while your house is listed for sale and make sure you are aware of and prepared for any showings.

SIX

GETTING AN OFFER

Seller Response...

When the time comes and you get an offer on your house, it is normal to be excited and have sweaty palms. Your agent, per the law, needs to notify you as soon as an offer comes in and forward and/or bring the offer to you as soon as possible. The phrase, *"time is of the essence"* is no joke in real estate. Remember at any point until you and the buyer have reached full mutual agreement, there is no deal and the buyer or you are free to walk away or make/take another offer.

Once a buyer submits an offer, you the seller will have a specified time period to review the offer and respond. The seller's review time period is usually stated on the first page of the offer and indicated as "Offer Expiration." Typically 9 p.m. (on the indicated offer expiration date) is when the buyer's offer is no longer valid. As the seller, you can do one of the following when you receive an offer.

1. Ignore the offer and never respond (technically you can't ignore it if it is full price and meets all of the stated terms in the posted listing).

2. Counter the buyer's offer.

3. Accept the buyer's offer.

If you accept the buyer's offer completely as is, making no changes at all to any of the stated terms then you will then have mutual agreement. Mutual agreement means all parties have agreed to and acknowledged the stated terms of the agreement and now the timelines and contingencies in the deal begin.

Any substantive change that you make to the buyer's offer is considered a counter offer. The buyer then has a review period to respond to your counter offer or to let it pass and thus the game ends. All changes on the offer paperwork should be acknowledged by both parties with their initials/dates. Including a date with all initialed changes may not always be legally necessary but to keep things clear and for best practice, a good listing agent is going to insist you date everything you sign or initial.

If something changed needs to be written out, it should be executed on a blank addendum or a counter offer form so that it is legible and clear to all parties before they acknowledge it. There is nothing more unprofessional and potentially confusing than when a seller or their agent hand scribbles in a change and submits that to a buyer as a counter offer; especially in today's world where online forms, online signings are accessible and easy to do. Keep it simple, keep it clear, and make it concise. If you do not understand a buyer's offer, then it is probably best to have a local real estate attorney explain it to you and/or revise the wording such that it is clear and legal. Your agent can execute very simple counter offer verbiage but if it begins to get complex or legal in any manner, it is best to have a local real estate attorney advise how you should word it. Your agent is not a real estate attorney and cannot practice law via the purchase and sale agreement's verbiage.

Your agent needs to be organized, timely, and available. He needs to know how to keep a paper trail of when your offer, counter offers are submitted, accepted or rejected. It can backfire on you big time, if your agent does not understand the importance of filing the paperwork and properly documenting it. Once your offer is mutually accepted, a good listing agent should change the status of the property in the MLS. It could go from active status to pending inspection or pending.

If for some reason you decide after you submit your counter offer and are awaiting the buyer's response that you no longer want to continue negotiating with this buyer (i.e. you are getting a better offer from another buyer), your agent should fill out a Withdrawal of Offer or Counter Offer Form 36A (in WA State) and submit that to the buyer's agent. Failing to do that in a timely manner, can mean you might get locked into a deal with the first buyer and have no means of getting out of it unless the buyer decides to walk. Therefore, I think it is best when you are going back and forth with counter offers, that you are sure you like the terms you are countering and/or agreeing to as you could very likely be legally bound to honor those terms. I also think it is best to stick with one offer at a time while countering back and forth; i.e. if your agent learns there is another buyer who now has interest in making an offer, it might be best to have them wait until you and the current buyer have completed your counter offer process and the counter offers have completely expired, then there is no way you can get locked in a deal with the first buyer.

Once you have reached mutual agreement (both parties have agreed to and acknowledged via their signatures all of the terms in the offer paperwork), the deal's contingency timelines come in to play. I provide my clients with an easy to follow timeline sheet that outlines when the specific contingencies in their deal expire, when certain tasks need to be completed, and important dates and deadlines to be aware of. I usually provide this sheet to escrow and the buyer's lender if they are interested. This way everyone knows at a quick glance when a specific deadline is for your transaction.

Offer Price...

Probably the first thing you are going to zoom in on when you receive an offer is the offer price. That is an important component but you still need to look over the other terms of the offer thoroughly with your listing agent and see what the whole sum total ends up being. When you listed your place, your agent should have provided you with the active and sold comparison data and that is hopefully how you arrived at your list price. Since listing, the market may have changed and your agent should provide you with updated active and sold comparison data. You need to evaluate that when you review the buyer's offer. If the buyer has a good buyer's agent, then that agent provided the buyer with the same active and sold comp data that you are looking at. This is what the buyer worked from, hopefully! Even if your home listed just a few days ago, the data on those sheets could have changed; the current state of the market is always in flux.

Look at your updated active and sold comp sheets. What do the statistics show you about the list price? When was the most recent sale on the comp sheet? Does the buyer's offer price fall within the range of what the active and sold comps show you?

From your perspective, the seller, you need to have a sense of the current state of the market and more specifically the state of the market where you are selling not in the whole metro or state region. What they tell you about your local real estate market on TV is not necessarily applicable. Typically the media reports on real estate trends that are peaking or fading. They tend to be a bit behind the reality of the current state of the market. Also, they usually are reporting in a broad brush sense. Meaning, they might be reporting on hot home sales within the city but where you are selling is, 30 minutes outside of the city in a bedroom community, the market conditions might not be as hot as in the city or vice-versa. Even more specific, what is the state of the market for your neighborhood? Some neighborhoods remain hot in down turns; others are slower, or faster than surrounding neighborhoods.

Other Terms...

As important as the buyer's offer price may be, you need to look over what the other terms of the offer are and put it all together and see what the end result is. Most buyers are going to have to have financing in order to buy your home. Therefore, there should be a Financing Addendum 22-A (in WA State) included with the buyer's offer. What type of loan is the buyer approved for, what are the timelines they are requesting in order for the lender to put together and fund the buyer's loan? Also, is the buyer requesting that you pay for any of her pre-paid items or closing costs? This could be quite a chunk of change, sometimes $5,000 or more. You need to realize that a full price offer, really isn't full price if you end up paying for any of the buyer's allowable closing costs. Therefore an offer that is not full price but does not request the seller pay any closing costs on the financing addendum may be something you prefer. Overall, it probably does not matter too much one way or the other, as you will focus on the bottom line of what you are going to walk away with, your net.

Here is a **tip**, remember that you are paying the selling office commission that is stated in your listing report on the actual sale price of your property not the sale price less any items you agree to pay for; i.e. the buyer's closing costs or pre-paid items, via the financing addendum. Unless your listing reports states that you are only paying a selling office commission on your actual net after any seller paid concessions have been paid, you are obligated to pay on the sale price. I run into this all the time when I am representing buyers. The listing agent tries to casually slip in our conversation when we are approaching the closing date, that of course the seller is only paying a selling office commission based on their actual net after the buyer's loan costs have been paid by the seller and/or the seller has paid for the agreed to repairs via the inspection contingency. Not bloody likely. The seller is legally obligated to pay the commission on the sale price. Just another item your listing agent should review with you prior to listing, so you do not have an unexpected surprise.

Another item to look over is the buyer's inspection contingency. How many days have they asked for to do their inspection? Those are days the buyer has to inspect your house and say yea or nay on going forward with the deal. The inspection contingency is the most common way a buyer uses to back out of a deal. Therefore, it is doubtful you want to give them an extended time frame to do their inspection. The usual time line where I practice is between five and seven days after mutual agreement. You need to also check the additional inspections clause and make sure that time line is reasonable as well. If the buyer's general inspector suggests they do an additional inspection (i.e. have an electrician evaluate a condition, etc…) then you want to make sure the buyer does not have too much time there to drag things out.

If your agent posted your completed seller disclosure statement online with your listing (and they should in my opinion), then the buyer should have signed off on the fifth page (in WA State) acknowledging receipt of that form. Typically they will then have a three day time period after mutual agreement to review the form and back out of the deal based on that review. Your agent should make sure this signed off page is submitted with the buyer's offer. The seller disclosure statement is not technically part of the purchase and sale agreement but the law does require the seller provide it to a buyer prior to the closing date (in WA State). Therefore, it is in your best interest to have this form back and signed by the buyer right off the bat. If your agent fails to get this form back from the buyer, then the buyer could technically terminate the deal all the way up to the closing day and get their earnest money deposit back. That does happen occasionally so a good listing agent is going to be pro-active with this form and make sure it is signed by the buyer and back ASAP.

If you counter a buyer's offer, please do not ask your agent to cross out certain verbiage in the standardized purchase and sale agreement forms. Your agent is not allowed to do that. They should not be altering any of those forms' boilerplate language as only a real estate attorney can do that. Your agent can craft very simple custom language in your counter offer via a blank addendum or the counter offer form but anything that is remotely complex or legal, requires a local real estate attorney to provide the correct wording.

Another item to mention when evaluating a buyer's offer, please do not show up drunk or stoned. You need to have your full wits about you. Party all you want, just do not mix it with your offer review time. The very first deal I ever wrote up, the man buying was old enough to be my grandfather. We sat down at the table to start the paperwork and he pulled a bottle of whiskey out of his blazer and proceeded to gulp it down. I can still see the younger version of myself standing there, trying to politely ask him to put the whiskey away, and to please come back later when he was sober to write up his offer. That is one of the advantages of getting older, because today I would not hesitate to boot him out and firmly tell him he needed to sober up first before writing up his offer. Reviewing a buyer's offer when you are buzzed or inebriated is not in your best interest, do not do it. And please do not sit down with your agent and hit the bottle or bong together when you are reviewing an offer. An agent is not supposed to be partying while they are working with a client.

CHARLES CHAPLIN
Low-Ball Offers...

Sometimes a seller will get a low-ball offer. By that I mean, you can see from the most recent active/sold comp statistics that your property's current market value is around the $300,000 and that is your list price. You receive an offer from a buyer of $245,000. Don't let that send your blood pressure soaring! First, in some parts of the country low-ball offers and then haggling over the purchase price is expected. That's not the case where I sell but again in certain markets that is how the game is played. A good buyer's agent is going to educate their client as to how things are usually done in your part of the country. Sometimes even if the buyer's agent has tried to educate his buyers, the buyers still might persist in submitting a low-ball offer. As I advise my buyers, usually this low-ball offer tactic backfires on them. Sometimes a buyer has to lose and learn via a low-ball offer and it unfortunately is on your shift to educate them as to how the game is played where you live.

You may be so annoyed with the low-ball offer that you want to throw it away and not bother responding at all. That is an option, but I would strongly advise taking a deep breath and then counter offer the buyer's ridiculous offer with your list price or close to it, as long as the most recent active and sold comps still back up your list price point.

A side note, your agent is the messenger for your offer. You run the show and decide what terms you will or will not accept in any offer and the terms of any counter offer you may make. You can ask for your agent's opinion but they should not be telling you what to do no questions asked. It is illegal for your agent to refuse to present your counter offer because she feels it is too low or there is something else she does not agree with you about in your counter offer. It has zero to do with how she feels or her ego. Your agent has to fill in the blanks per your instruction (unless you are instructing her to break the law) and present your counter offer.

Multiple Offers...

If the market is hot when you are selling and the housing inventory is low and lots of people are buying, then you are in a seller's market and more than likely there are going to be multiple offers. Multiple offers means that more than one person is making an offer on your property. How this can work is the seller, via their listing agent, will state (usually in the online listing report) something like, *"Seller to review all offers, if any, on Thursday, March 15 at 5 p.m."* This is a case where your agent will need to post a letter on file from you stating this is what you have instructed them to do for offers. Posting such verbiage in your listing report does not guarantee you are going to get multiple offers it just sets up the rules for such a scenario in advance. You also need to decide if you want to state that buyers should make their best offer right off the bat or if you are going to allow for escalations, via the Escalation Addendum 35E (in WA State). This form is submitted with the buyer's offer and it details how much over a competing offer's best price the buyer is willing to go in order to get the property. Typically escalations are in $1,000 or more increments and the buyer indicates their escalation price cap. For example, a buyer's offer is for the list price of $320,000 and their escalation clause

131

is for $1,000 over any competing offers up to $350,000. They beat out the competing offer and the purchase price ends up being $346,000. The listing agent has to provide the buyer's agent a complete copy of the closest competing offer, per the terms of the escalation addendum, to verify that $346,000 is correct and the closest offer maxed out at $345,000. A **tip**, never be tempted to ask your agent to fake or pretend with a buyer's agent that there is another competing offer. That is illegal and with the required documentation, you will get caught. No ethical or smart listing agent is going to do this or agree to this, as they could lose their license for doing so; don't go there!

When a buyer's agent is putting together an offer for a buyer in a multiple offer situation these are some of the usual things a smart agent will advise doing to make his buyer's offer more seller friendly.

1. He may suggest his buyer do a pre-inspection on your home. You the seller have to give permission for this. This is where one or more buyers may want access to your house prior to making their offers on Thursday and they will be paying to have their inspectors inspect the house in advance. This way they will know the condition of your home ahead of time and can therefore not include an inspection contingency when making their offer. This might be something you prefer. Once the offer is mutually agreed upon, there is no inspection contingency hoop to wait around and jump through. The deal is straight on its way to appraisal and closing.

2. A buyer may increase their earnest money deposit (explained in minute). This is more of a psychological ploy but it can look good on paper.

3. They may increase their down payment.

4. They most likely will tighten up all of the contingency timelines, i.e. their financing timeline if possible.

5. They may not ask the seller to pay for any of their allowable pre-paid or closing cost items via their financing addendum.

6. If the comps show the list price is close to where it should be, they most likely will offer full list price. Obviously they may not do this if the list price is overinflated, via the comps.

7. They will probably not include a three day neighborhood review contingency.

8. They should sign off on the seller disclosure statement (if it is properly filled out) such that they waive their right to terminate their offer based on a three day review of it.

9. They may write a personalized letter to you as a ploy to win favor. Hopefully what they submit is not too over the top rainbows and unicorns.

Earnest Money Deposit...

What is an Earnest Money Deposit (EMD)? An EMD is the amount of money the buyer pledges such that if they do not fulfill their end of the contract and pull out of the deal for no legal reason, then the seller is going to keep a portion or all of the EMD as compensation for wasting their time. In reality, the EMD is somewhat of a formality and it is pretty hard to collect it unless the buyer just flakes out on the deal for no legal reason and there are no more contingencies left for them to legally terminate the deal.

It appears that earnest money deposits came into play during 1980s. Prior to the EMD being used, buyers would sometimes write up offers simultaneously on several houses and then make up their mind later on as to which one they wanted. So they would get three offers accepted and then later on back out of two of the deals. This was unfair to sellers and using an EMD with each offer helped to stop this. The EMD was created most likely by a savvy agent who wanted the sellers to take his buyer's offer seriously. So they pledged a certain amount of money to show their offer was "earnest" not a frivolous offer that could easily be withdrawn on whim. EMD took off and to my knowledge most residential transactions in the United States have some form of EMD involved. Where I practice, it is expected and if a buyer's agent submits an offer without an earnest money promissory note or a copy of the buyer's EMD check attached, you can count on any smart listing agent advising the seller not to consider the offer until that is taken care of.

Traditionally when a buyer meets to write up their offer they make out a check to the buyer's brokerage or to the indicated escrow company for their earnest money deposit. The old school "rule" in the Seattle metro area was that the expected earnest money deposit was typically three percent of the list price. It got as high as five percent during the boom for certain areas. Then a copy of the buyer's EMD check is submitted with the offer. This has been the traditional way of handling the EMD.

However, today many buyers and agents are now meeting online to write up the offer, via an electronic signature verification service which many MLS and state laws now accept as okay for real estate transactions (verify this for your state). In Washington State via the NWMLS, this service is Authentisign. This in fact may be how you and your listing agent are going to initially review an offer, together online. This is a practice that appears to be growing and is popular.

Since many buyers and their agents are not meeting in person to write up an offer, then they will most likely use an Earnest Money Promissory Note Form 31 (in WA State). This note binds the buyer to make the agreed upon earnest money deposit at a later date. It is a legal substitute for the check's hard copy is one way of looking at it. Many agents who meet with their clients in person to write up an offer are now using the earnest money promissory note instead of collecting a hard copy EMD check right away. There are now stricter laws in play (in WA State) as to who has to hold the EMD check, how long before it has to be delivered to escrow or the brokerage and deposited. Thus, some agents and brokerages now prefer that a buyer write out and deliver the EMD check directly to escrow.

Common sense, when it is more of a buyer's market then the EMD amount usually diminishes. When it is a seller's market, or a multiple offer situation, the EMD typically increases. It is really purely psychological but that is how the game is usually played. When the EMD is delivered, per the terms of the purchase and sale agreement, to the designated escrow office (more on escrow later), then escrow cashes it and holds it until your settlement/closing goes through. A good listing agent knows per the purchase and sale agreement when the earnest money deposit is due and will always request a receipt of this deposit from the buyer's agent or escrow and provide you with a copy of it for your records.

If the buyer terminates the deal, per the stated terms in the purchase and sale agreement, and their agent files the appropriate paperwork they will get their EMD refunded. Escrow will require certain signed forms from both parties be submitted first before they will write a check and refund the buyer's EMD. One of the most common ways for a buyer to get their EMD back is if they do their inspection and discover that there are way more issues with your house than they bargained for. Their agent will submit the 35R Inspection Response Form (in WA State) and their EMD will be refunded if it was filed properly and on time.

All Cash and 22EF...

If you are fortunate, you may get a buyer who is flush with cash and wants to pay all cash for your property. Their offer will obviously not be contingent on financing. However, your agent will need to ensure an evidence of funds, funds availability, is provided with the buyer's offer. They can also use (in WA State) the 22EF Evidence of Funds Addendum with their offer. This form spells out timelines for the buyer to provide the above mentioned funds availability letter. Also, this form is used if the buyer is paying all cash via a gift or from the proceeds they will have from the sale of a property they currently own and are selling.

Savvy listing agents have also started to require the Evidence of Funds form 22EF be used to verify that a potential buyer in fact has the required non-contingent funds necessary to close the deal. The loan pre-approval letter is verifying that a loan person has reviewed a buyer's situation and has pre-approved them for a loan of X amount. This letter does not state that the loan person has verified that the buyer has the necessary cash available to pay for her down payment. Non-contingent funds would most likely be the down payment. So in an offer, the financing contingency form states the buyer is doing a conventional first mortgage and the pre-approval letter verifies this. The financing contingency form also shows the buyer is doing a 20% down payment. That 20% has most likely not been verified by the lender and certainly the lender's pre-approval letter does not state it has.

Therefore, the buyer needs to have that 20% available in cash in a savings account, investment account, a gift from someone, etc.... This all needs to be verified up front. Hence, smart listing agents are now requiring buyers submit the 22EF form with their offer and with that form submit proof verifying funds are available to cover the down payment or other non-contingent funds that are required to close the deal. Usually a buyer will submit a copy of their most recent savings account statement and hopefully their agent will white out their account number (for fraud protection). But the buyer's name, financial institution and date of the statement should be visible and of course

CHARLES CHAPLIN

the required amount of money to complete the deal should show as on deposit and available for use.

Updated Pre-Approval Letter...

If the buyers are making an offer contingent upon financing, then your agent should make sure a pre-approval certificate/letter is included with the offer paperwork. You and your agent should look over the terms and your agent may want to contact this loan person directly to verify it is in fact legitimate. The buyer's loan person should not give away private information about the buyer or let your agent know how high the buyer's total loan pre-approval is for.

A few years back I was the listing agent and a buyer submitted an offer on my seller's house. Their agent had most of the offer paperwork filled out correctly but they submitted the buyer's original pre-approval letter that was a two months old. It clearly stated the buyer was pre-approved for a $425,000 loan and that was not based on the seller paying any allowable closing costs or pre-paid items for the buyer. The list price of my client's house was $375,000 and the buyer's offer price was $368,000 with the buyer asking the seller to pay their closing costs of something like $4,500. Had their loan person updated their pre-approval letter and their agent submitted their offer with the offer specific loan pre-approval letter, we would have had no clue that the buyer's pre-approval was for over $368,000 and that the buyer's pre-approval was not contingent upon the seller paying for the buyer's pre-paid items and closing costs. Thanks to their lack of attention to detail, my seller knew the buyer's hand. Thus, the seller countered back at full list price with the seller not paying any of the buyer's closing costs. The buyer accepted that counter. I never figured out if the buyer had any idea that the un-updated, loan pre-approval letter submitted with his offer gave his hand away. Based on the stories I hear, this kind of sloppy work is not that uncommon.

Another one I recently heard, a listing agent contacted the buyer's loan person and verified the pre-approval letter was okay for the offer on hand. The loan person then volunteered to the listing agent that the buyer was pre-approved for quite a bit more money and when the listing agent asked, the lender replied that the buyer did not have to have the seller pay for the buyer's closing costs as the offer requested. This gave the seller a huge advantage when they wrote their counter offer for full list price with the seller paying zero of the buyer's closing costs. Again with this story, whether the buyer had any clue their loan person threw them under the bus by providing the listing agent with way too much information is anyone's guess!

Reviewing the Estimated Seller's Net Proceeds...

When you first met with your agent and filled out the listing paperwork, you should have reviewed an estimated seller's net proceeds sheet. This sheet should have estimated what your approximate net would be at the given list price minus your mortgage pay-off, all commissions, title and closing fees and taxes. Where I practice, a good ball park estimate for what the seller ends up paying is around 9% of the sale price. That is probably a bit high, but better to estimate more than less! Different parts of the country will have different estimate percentages as the fees and taxes of course vary. When you review an offer from a buyer, you and your agent should also review that ball park percentage times the offer price, less any additional seller paid concessions the buyer may have requested via their financing addendum. You also need to anticipate any repair work cost requests that may come from the buyer's inspection. That is not always easy to do, but something to keep in mind before you sign off and agree to an offer.

An example of this would be the offer price is $300,000 and the estimated seller costs are approximately 9%. Thus the estimated cost for listing and selling equals $27,000. If you accept an offer of $300,000 then your estimated seller net is $273,000; assuming you own your home free and clear and have no mortgages or equity lines of credit on your home that have to be paid off at closing. You already know the hot water tank is over 20 years old and it is likely a buyer's inspector is going to suggest replacing it. There is a good chance the buyer will request you replace the hot water tank prior to closing via their inspection repair request. You think that might be something you the seller will pay in order to keep the deal afloat. So you budget ahead and anticipate spending around $1,000 for the hot water tank purchase and installation (you will want to verify via local contractors in your areas to estimate costs). Therefore, in this case you are now estimating that your net will be around $272,000. However, you are aware that other items may be revealed during the inspection and there may be additional unknown costs.

The times to review your estimated seller's set proceeds sheet are:

1. Before you list your home for sale.

2. When you receive an offer.

3. After a buyer's inspection, should any repair requests be submitted for your consideration.

4. At your signing appointment, before your closing date.

Real Life...

Years ago, I had a listing with a seller who was on the road nonstop. We barely had time to do our listing appointment and get things set up before he was off on the road for business again. This man was literally on the road and traveling for business over 330 days out of the year and had been doing this for decades. He was wealthy and owned several houses scattered around the globe which he rarely frequented. The one he listed with me was very nice. He had a service that maintained the grounds and checked the interior weekly as well as prep the property for him to stay in on the rare occasions he was in town. At the start, I recognized tracking this man down for any buyer questions or offers was going to be a challenge. He had an entire staff of official assistants. In fact, he had one of his assistants meet with me initially to show me the house he wanted to list and sell. He was a very nice in person, just busy and never available. I asked if he could appoint a local attorney to act on his behalf, via a power of attorney, to review any offers when they came in. I realized tracking him down and getting an offer in front of him to review and actually properly sign was going to be an issue. This was prior to agents having access to companies like Authentisign whereby he could review an offer online and click the indicated blanks for his signatures and acceptance. However, even if that kind of option had been around back then, I

141

doubt he would have had the patience and time to review an offer online and sign electronically.

Unfortunately he was not in favor of appointing anyone to act on his behalf. So any offers would have to be overnighted to him and I would have to try and have the offer expiration be for several days later so as to accommodate the seller's busy schedule. Buyers are never very thrilled with that scenario but this was the best I could do in this situation. Sure enough, a good offer came in and it took me and the assistants two days to track down the seller. We would think we found him only to discover he was on a plane to another city. By the time the offer reached him it had expired and the buyer's agent let me know they were moving on to another property. This happened again with a new buyer and this time the offer reached the seller but he failed to sign all the required papers and return them. That offer fell apart as well. At that point the seller realized that my power of attorney suggestion might be a better way to approach this. We did get a local attorney to agree and the next offer went through the attorney who reviewed and signed things for the seller and we reached mutual agreement. We did the same fire drill for the inspection requests. The deal closed and it was literally a year later before I could reach the former owner and give him a thank you gift for listing with me.

Not everyone is as busy as Mr. Globe Trotter but still it is very important to make sure your agent can reach you at all times and that you are able to respond to any offers right away. It's easier today because of technology advances but still something you and your agent need to discuss and plan for in advance.

SEVEN

MUTUAL AGREEMENT

Buyer's Inspection...

Any educated buyer is going to have their offer include an inspection contingency. So your deal's paperwork will most likely include the Inspection Contingency Form 35 (in WA State). The norm where I sell for a residential inspection time period is usually five to seven days, sometimes up to 10 days after mutual agreement occurs. Usually the inspection time period is fairly short, because you do not want to tie up your property for too long, via the inspection contingency. A buyer might do their inspection and decide to terminate the deal and move on. From your perspective, you want to know sooner, rather than later if the buyer is going to proceed with the transaction. Getting the inspection contingency out of the way is one of the best indicators you have that the buyer is moving forward with the deal.

Also, the buyer's lender is not going to want to wait forever to hear back about whether or not their inspection is complete and they are moving ahead with the deal. The lender usually wants to hold off on ordering the appraisal (more on that later) for the property until they know the buyer's inspection contingency is satisfied.

In Washington State, all home inspectors must be licensed and your agent may provide you with an Inspector Referral Disclosure Form 41-D which lists any home inspectors your agent is either related to or who have been hired by the agent to inspect a property the agent is personally purchasing.

The buyer's agent should let your agent know when the buyer has scheduled their home inspection; i.e. Tuesday the 14th at 2:00 p.m. If for some reason that date and time do not work for you, you will need to let your agent know immediately so the buyer can reschedule. However, it is usually best if you can rearrange things to make the buyer's scheduled inspection appointment work. You want to keep things friendly especially before they set their inspector loose on your house! You will need to leave the property while the buyer, their agent and inspector have a look at things. The average inspection is usually between one to two hours, longer if your house is large; all day if you own an enormous estate, sometimes two! You can ask the buyer's agent to call you on your cell phone to let you know they are finished. The buyer's agent is present to get the keys, unlock the house and make sure the buyer and their posse of people do not break or steal anything. They are required by law to remain on site for the entire inspection, or else have a licensed assistant or another licensed agent be there. The inspector should be checking for things that are visible and accessible, they can't knock holes in the walls, remove siding, etc.... They are going to want access to everything; attics, crawl spaces, permanent storage sheds, garage, etc.... If any of those require extra keys or special access instructions you need to leave that for them. The easier you can make their inspection, hopefully the better it will go. If there is anything special you think they should know, such as the crawl space door sticks or how to operate your programmable thermostat, then note that as well. Their inspector should be checking all the appliances that are included in the sale and will check central air, the hot water tank, electrical panel box. If your electrical panel box is hidden (covered over with a painting) please remove it so the panel box is easy to locate. Do not try to hide any defects as that will certainly work against you in many ways! If there has been any recent repair work to the house that is noted on your seller disclosure statement, you may want to leave copies of those detailed, paid-in-full, invoices out so the inspector and buyer can review them.

If you live in an older house, there is a good chance the buyer is going to pay to have a sewer scoping company scope the sewer line. They will be checking to make sure the sewer pipe from your house to the street is connected, and working properly. They do this by putting a camera scope down the line and filming it from the street to your house. If something is found to be wrong there, that is definitely something you are going to have to have fixed either prior to closing or if this buyer terminates the deal, you will need to have that addressed before another buyer shows up and note this on an updated seller disclosure statement. Technically, you could just note what was found wrong with your sewer line but even in a hot seller's market it is highly doubtful a buyer is going to pay to repair your sewage line and their lender will typically not fund their loan unless it is repaired.

Other items that might be found by the general inspector would be a hot water tank that is past its replacement date, a dishwasher that does not work, electrical issues that need to be addressed, etc.... The buyer frequently will ask the seller to repair these kinds of things. Just remember if you do not agree to any requested repairs and the buyer walks, then you will need to revise your seller disclosure statement to include those items that the buyer's inspector called or you could pay to have your own inspector look at those items and see what his opinion is. Probably it would be best to address them and move on but a local real estate attorney should advise you on how to proceed. You do need to be prepared for the bombshell inspection. This is when a buyer's inspector discovers your house's foundation has serious issues or major support beams are failing, your house is sliding off the hill, etc.… These are huge items and when they occur it can be a very expensive shock. Usually in these cases the buyer terminates the deal. You will then probably want to take your home temporarily off the market while you have the situation assessed by your own people and then pay to have it corrected. Once you have had the foundation repaired or new support beams put in, you can then put your house back on the market but your seller disclosure statement will need to be revised to reflect the conditions that were discovered and repaired. Any new buyer is going to want to see the invoices and make sure the serious repair work was actually done and is now okay.

Inspection Response…

In Washington State, the buyer will do their inspection and then before their inspection contingency timeline expires, they should submit to your agent the Response For Form 35 (Form 35R). Form 35R provides the buyer's response to the seller after they have completed their inspection (via the Inspection Contingency Form 35).

The buyer will indicate one of the following on the 35R: they are okay with their inspection findings and are now waving the inspection contingency; they did not like the inspection results and are terminating the deal (requesting their earnest money deposit be returned); they are requesting repairs or modifications from the seller.

Assuming they ask for a couple of items to be repaired and you indicate in your response portion of the 35R that you agree to take care of those items, then the 35R is signed around and the inspection contingency is satisfied. If the buyer requests certain items be repaired prior to closing, via the 35R, then their agent and their loan person are going to need written verification from you that those items were completed and paid for. You should provide your agent with the repair invoices marked paid-in-full and she should forward those to the buyer's agent and to escrow.

Occasionally, a loan person's underwriter might require a condition that was repaired be re-inspected and confirm it is now okay. An example of this would be the house's roof needs to be replaced prior to closing. The 35R had that as a condition and you agreed to replace the roof. The buyer's agent collects the roof replacement, receipt marked paid-in-full, and he and the buyer visually verify the work was done during their final walk through of the property (five days prior to closing in WA State). If the loan underwriter is picky, they may require the buyer have their original inspector go back out and verify in writing that the roof was replaced and is now okay.

Home Buyer Warranty...

Your agent hopefully made you aware of home buyer warranties and what they are when you met for your initial meeting. Usually a home buyer warranty will insure the systems in a property that you are selling for a set period of time after you sell. For example, your home was built in 1980 and the furnace and appliances are from that year as well. If you have a home buyer warranty policy in place, then if the furnace needs replacing or the old dish washer dies six months after you sell, the home buyer warranty will usually cover some of the costs to replace those failed items. Different companies offer different levels of coverage, have varying lengths of time and price points. I advise clients to learn more about the different home buyer warranty companies and available warranties prior to listing their house. Occasionally, buyers will request the seller purchase one of these for them as a condition of their offer or will request via their inspection response form. Sometimes sellers will offer a home buyer warranty as a buying incentive. Many transactions do not have home buyer warranties involved but it is something you as a seller should know about prior to listing.

Appraisal...

Once your deal is mutually accepted, the buyer's loan person should receive a complete copy of the signed around deal from the buyer's real estate agent. A good listing agent will verify that this has happened. The loan person can then start to set things up and get the ball rolling on the buyer's financing. Usually, a loan person likes to wait until the inspection contingency has been removed to order the appraisal. The appraiser is an independent party contracted by the buyer's lender via a random lottery assignment system. In the past, lenders were allowed to cherry pick which appraisers they worked with and contracted to evaluate property values. This led to some cases of collusion. Thus, the laws changed and now appraisers are randomly assigned. The appraiser is trained and licensed to evaluate property and ensure that the lender is loaning money for a viable commodity (no Brooklyn Bridges or phantom homes) and that the price the buyer is paying for the property is of fair market value. Fair market value means the sale price is congruent with other similar sales. In other words, the buyer is not over paying (they are not over lending) for the purchase of your house. In a hot and increasing market, when values of homes can literally shoot up over night, the appraiser has to be more diligent due to the rapidly accelerating market conditions. What seemed overpriced last week may now be the new going rate. The appraiser is going to visit the property and check it out in person and she is going to pull active and sold comparison reports, just like the ones you hopefully used when you determined what offer price to accept. The buyer and their agent do not attend the appraisal, nor does your agent. The appraiser usually has their own key box access and they should contact you and your agent to schedule a date and time to come out and do the appraisal. It is best if you leave the property while the appraiser is there. You can leave any special instructions for the appraiser, but it is usually best if you leave. They can call you when they are done. The appraiser will need full access to everything just like what you did for the buyer's inspection. It might not be as thorough as the buyer's inspection but the appraiser does measure all rooms and check for certain conditions, per the requirements of the buyer's loan type.

If for some reason the appraisal of your property is under what the agreed upon purchase price is then you and the buyer will have to revisit the deal to see what can be done. Your purchase and sale agreement's financing addendum should spell out the fire drill that occurs should an appraisal come in under the purchase price. In Washington State that is Form 22-A and the options for the seller per the buyer's written notice that the appraisal is low are for the seller to give notice that:

1. Seller is going to pay for another appraisal of the property by the same appraiser or another appraiser that is approved by the buyer's lender. This could be a long shot, i.e. trying to get the appraised value raised and even if you are successful it is still contingent upon the buyer's lender accepting your revised appraisal.

2. Seller agrees to reduce the sale price of the property to an amount not exceeding what the buyer's appraiser says the house is worth. The buyer's lender must agree to this. If the buyer's lender does agree then the buyer is bound to complete the deal (unless they are purchasing via a FHA, VA, RD loan).

3. Seller can reject the notice from the buyer of a low appraisal. The buyer then has a set time period to waive his financing contingency or terminate the deal

and have their earnest money deposit refunded. The buyer's lender is going to require the buyer's appraisal come in okay in order for their loan to fund. So essentially, either the purchase price is reduced so the buyer's appraisal is okay or the deal is most likely over. This is a very basic outline of what happens if a property does not appraise and each case is unique. You should always consult with a local real estate attorney for advice as to how best proceed in this situation or for detailed information as to what the verbiage pertaining to this situation in your purchase and sale agreement exactly means.

Real Life...

A few years back a friend's mother who was getting up there in years, suddenly decided to purchase a condominium in a retirement community with progressive care service options and to list and sell her current house. My friend had no idea this was even happening until she was informed after the fact. The friend then contacted me for my opinion on the situation and.

Her mother was approaching 85 and was still mentally capable, drove her car, was living independently and quite active socially. She really did not have a reason at the moment to move out of her current house. The current house was a one story, Frank Lloyd Wright style house with no steps or stairs. It was not too large and she had help who came three times a week to clean and assist her with weekly tasks. The yard was not enormous and there too she had a yard service that kept it neatly maintained. Money was not an issue, so why this sudden decision to list and sell and move into a retirement community?

Turns out, mommy's good friend, Steve, was an agent. This man was in his early 70s and had Santa Clause charm in spades. He took my friend's mother out to parties, played bridge with her set of friends and appeared to be a nice person to know. He was retired from his former career as an architect and had been selling real estate as a side line for about ten years. One day he suggested to my friend's mother that they should stop by a local retirement community that had new condominiums for sale. He toured the compound with her and the site agent for the community was all smiles and said she could probably get my friend's mother in one of the larger units if she was quick. The larger units were apparently almost all sold out, in fact only one was left. Steve then put the squeeze on mommy; yes she was active and capable now but what if she had a fall or needed assistance sometime soon (one never knows when disaster can strike)? Didn't she want to think ahead, be pro-active and not be an undue burden on her adult children? This community was great, she could have her large condominium unit and still live independently and then as she aged, they had progressive care and other living options. Mommy agreed, and signed on the dotted line right there on site; she didn't want to miss out on the last large unit that was for sale.

Once she had signed on to purchase one of these not inexpensive condos and paid the required one hundred thousand dollar entry fee required to buy something in this retirement community, the next step for Steve was to list her current house for sale and get it sold ASAP. He did just that, the very next day her place was listed for sale and on the market. My friend's mother never saw any active or sold comparison reports to show her what her current house was actually worth. Steve assured her the list price was accurate and had his for sale sign in her yard within days. This is when my friend learned about all of this. Her mother was very stressed out and moving at the speed of lightening to sell her house and move into the new retirement community. The woman who helped her a few times a week actually called the daughter to let her know what was going on and to tell her that her mother was so frazzled that she had not been sleeping for days.

I got a call and took a look at the retirement community paperwork, what little of it they had provided her mother a copy of. It was outrageous. The fees, the non refundable "deposit" and buried in their boilerplate verbiage it stated that if and when her mother actually needed medical care or round the clock nursing assistance, there was no guarantee that a room would be available in their onsite medical care facility. In fact, that facility was in my opinion, way too small to accommodate the potential for need given the community's size. I later found out online that this was a huge criticism of this retirement living community; people who paid huge fees to live there and then when they actually needed the care they had supposedly paid the big fees for, there was no room available and they were on their own and actually out of there.

The next red flag for me was the contract's resale verbiage. Here, the retirement community controlled everything. So when a resident passed away, the heirs to their property essentially have no rights. The community's board decides what the list price for the unit's resale will be, requires only one of their approved real estate agents list it and at a minimum they take sixty percent off any profit or gain that is made when the unit is resold. Then there are all the fees they require an heir to pay when the unit sells. I thought it was a huge rip-off and it looked to me like their goal was to empty the pockets of all retirees living there so that once they passed away there would hardly be a penny left for the heirs. This was another complaint I read about this facility online.

I put my friend in touch with a real estate attorney in her area and they set to work to undo this. Steve had not technically violated any licensing laws but it was clear as bell to everyone that his agenda was to make as much money off her mother as quickly as possible. Since this friend's mother was fully competent, there was no legal way to get her out of her purchase at the retirement community based on being mentally deficient or pressured and tricked into purchasing. Luckily, her mother had the good sense to insist that they allow her to have an inspection contingency in her offer/purchase once the construction of this unit was final. Her paperwork did state that upon written notice from the community's developer that this unit's construction was complete; the buyer would have seven days to do any inspections and approve it. When this information got to the real estate attorney, the notice of completion had already been provided to the mother and there were two days left for her to back out based on the inspection contingency clause. That's what they used to get her mother out of this deal.

For her house, things were more difficult. She had already accepted an offer and the buyer's inspection was done. Things were proceeding to closing and she was obligated to sell. Fortunately for her, it turns out the appraisal came in below the agreed to sale price. She gave notice to the buyer rejecting their low appraisal and since the buyer's lender was not going to be able to make the deal happen unless they both agreed to a lower sale price, the buyer had to terminate. This does not happen too often so this woman was extremely lucky. She was not as fortunate in recovering the entire non refundable "deposit" fee from the retirement community. I actually contacted the site agent there and learned that there were plenty of new larger condominium units still available for sale. So she and Steve had created a false sense of urgency to pressure my friend's mother into buying right away. This is sleazy but not unfortunately that uncommon. If you are elderly please do not be insulted if your listing agent asks you to involve one of your adult children and/or a local real estate attorney in your sale. The agent may state that any offer you receive needs to be reviewed by these parties. It is not meant to be insulting to you, it just makes wise consumer sense and could help you avoid a situation like this story illustrates.

EIGHT

CLOSING

Final Walk Through...

P er your purchase and sale agreement usually the buyer has the right to access your property prior to closing to recheck the property condition and verify any work orders via their inspection contingency have been addressed. In Washington State, the buyer will have a final walk through access five days prior to the stated closing date. The buyer and their agent will most likely want to stop by and revisit, so be aware. This is why it is important that any repair items you agree to address are taken care of by this final walk through date. If something has not been done by that date, then a good buyer's agent is going to notify escrow and suggest to their buyer that they not attend a signing appointment until your seller contractual obligations have been met. A good listing agent is going to remind the seller to make sure they have taken care of any repair work prior to the final walk through date and will want to collect all invoices/warranty copies from them marked "paid-in-full." He should forward those to the buyer's agent and to escrow.

Escrow...

The escrow officer is a neutral third party that acts like a referee in your transaction. They work per the stated terms of your purchase and sale agreement and the lender's instructions. Escrow does not advocate for you the seller or for the buyer. They are there to make sure the money in your deal is applied and disbursed properly and the deed is recorded in the buyer's name with the county recording office. The escrow officer needs to be organized, knowledgeable and able to get the deal closed. Some escrow officers are better than others. It is always completely at the client's discretion and choice which escrow company they want to use. An agent should always ask if the choice for the escrow company indicated on an offer is indeed the escrow company you wish to use. If you do not know much about escrow, then ask your agent if she has an escrow company she prefers to work with. That is no guarantee things will go smoothly but it does not hurt. The seller does not have to agree to use the escrow company that a buyer requests. Occasionally there are split escrows, where the seller has one escrow company and the buyer has another escrow company. That can make things a bit more confusing but it can be done.

Your agent (if they are organized) is going to get a complete copy of your deal paperwork to escrow as soon as you have mutual agreement. Escrow will then get your information, the buyer's information, and note the closing date. They will contact you at some point prior to the closing date to let you know what (if any) information they need from you. Escrow will usually need all of the buyer's loan documents from their loan person before they can set up your signing appointment. In some states, known as traditional closing states, you have a concurrent signing appointment and closing. Meaning, you and the buyer go to the escrow office on the closing date and sign the final paperwork together and the keys are given to the buyer then and there.

In Washington State that does not happen as they are what is known as an escrow state, there is a gap between signing and closing (usually two to three days). You will set up a signing appointment with escrow, usually a few days prior to your stated closing date. The buyer will have their own signing appointment. Once you have signed, you are still the owner and the keys will not be given to the buyer until escrow notifies all parties that the deed has recorded and the deal is closed.

The buyer's loan person is going to make sure that the appraisal is in and is okay. She (or her processor) will collect any other outstanding items from the buyer and then submit all of their loan paperwork, including a copy of the signed around deal to the underwriter. The underwriter then reviews everything. They may request additional information or not. Once the loan underwriter is okay, they will release the loan documents and forward them to the escrow company. Escrow will organize all of the buyer's loan documents, and prepare a settlement statement. This statement will itemize all expenses and credits for the seller and buyer on a master spreadsheet. You will only see the settlement statement for your half; you will not see the buyer's information.

The escrow officer is going to have you come in for your signing appointment. If it is two of you selling together and both names are on the title and the purchase and sale agreement paperwork, then you both need to attend a signing appointment. If for some reason the person you are selling with is not going to be available for a signing appointment, then you will need to have a power of attorney letter drawn up in advance and notarized which gives you the legal right to sign for the other party. That can be a bit of a pain to arrange, so it is best if each person who is on title as a seller (owner) be available to sign.

Signing Appointment...

At signing, you are going to review the settlement statement to ensure it makes sense and that the numbers there jive with what your estimated seller's net proceeds sheet showed you. Sometimes that estimate of costs is a bit over or under and what you will see on the settlement statement. If there are any questions or issues, then escrow will contact the appropriate person directly with questions. The escrow officer will have already told you prior to the signing appointment, what certified funds (if any) you will need to bring to your signing appointment and what form of photo identification they are going to need from you. Please make sure your identification is still valid. You do not want to be racing around to the DMV and trying to renew your expired driver's license during the mad rush to your closing date.

After the existing mortgage, commissions, fees, and taxes are paid, escrow will ask you at your signing appointment how you want your net gain disbursed to you; i.e. via a check or direct wire into your bank account? And they will let you know when that will be issued.

Once you have signed and the buyer has completed their signing appointment, then escrow will bundle up all of the buyer's loan documents and courier them back to their loan person's underwriter. The underwriter will do a final review of all the documents. Once they are satisfied that all is good, they will release the funds for the buyer's loan(s). Once escrow is notified that the buyer's loan has funded, they will make sure the deed is recorded with the county in the buyer's name. Escrow will then contact all parties to let them know the deal is now officially closed. At that point, your agent can give the house keys to the buyer's agent. No sane listing or buyer's agent is going to provide keys to a buyer until they have been notified directly by escrow that your deal is closed and the deed is now recorded in your name.

No Access...

Prior to your closing date, the buyer should not ask if they can store items in your vacant garage or have their new appliances installed in the kitchen. They do not own the property until it has recorded in their name. Therefore, you should never allow a buyer to leave/store their personal items at your property or make any changes to your house until you are notified by escrow that the buyer is now the new owner. Even if the house is vacant, it is not yet the buyer's. Prior to closing, what if you allow a buyer to put tools and some boxed items in your garage and they get stolen, or the garage burns down? Guess who is liable for the buyer's possessions that are stored at your house? You are! In your parents day these kinds of informal arrangements of storing items in a garage until closing were not so atypical. However, in today's litigious environment these arrangements should not happen. Another example of this, the house is empty, *"Does the seller mind if I go ahead and have the interior repainted prior to closing?"* Yes because there is liability on the seller's end and what if the deal does not close for some unforeseen reason? Prior to closing, a buyer should not start pruning the bushes or cutting down the tree they do not like.

160

Closing Plus Three…

As previously mentioned, in the old days it was not too uncommon to have your closing date stated as, *"Closing plus three."* This meant the closing date was say March 31 and so the buyer became the legal owner on the 31st but then they allowed you to remain in the property for three days after closing so you could move out. That is all but gone now. For good reason, i.e. the liability issues I just described and then some! There were many issues with what happens if the former owner damages the property during those three days, who is legally on the hook for repairs, what about injuries, etc…. There was usually no formal rental or lease agreement for those three days and thus the legal gray area was enormous. The law suits must have mounted regarding this issue because in Washington State that *"closing plus three"* option box was removed several years ago from the NWMLS purchase and sale agreement forms. A buyer most likely would not want to agree to *"closing plus three"* because why would he want a seller in his property for three days after closing?

If for whatever reason you need to do a leaseback option with the buyer, i.e. you want to close on the property and then rent it back from the buyer for a week or a month while you move out or you want to remain living there until your child's school year ends, then you absolutely want to have a local real estate attorney create a rental agreement for you to cover this. It should specify how damages will be handled, what kind of security deposit will be in play, who is going to hold that deposit in escrow, who is responsible for which utilities, and all the other items a normal apartment rental contract covers. Due to

161

stricter landlord/tenant laws, I highly doubt a buyer is going to agree to do a formal leaseback with you. Legally, your real estate agent and the listing agent should have no part in drafting this lease contract or in negotiating its terms and conditions.

Closing Day...

Your closing day will be clearly stated in your purchase and sale agreement. This is the date that the parties are agreeing title and ownership of the property will be transferred and recorded. Your closing day will never be on a legal holiday or a Saturday or Sunday. Sometimes your closing date has to be extended because the buyer's lender needs more time to close the loan. To extend the closing date, both parties must first agree to this in writing. In rare cases, a title condition hereto unknown may be discovered literally on closing day and cause the closing to be delayed. Also, the contract usually states the sellers are allowed to occupy the property until 9 p.m. of the closing day.

You are going to want to pack up, move out and then have the house cleaned prior to the buyer becoming the owner. There is a risk that you will do all of this and then right before or on the closing day, things fall apart and the deal dies. This is especially true if at the last minute the buyer's lender cannot fund the loan and thus game over. If the buyer's financing contingency has not been waived then they are entitled to a refund of their earnest money deposit. If your listing agent had you fill out and file a Financing Contingency Notice 22AR (in WA State) at the appropriate time (indicated on the financing addendum) then the buyer's financing contingency was waived or you had the right to terminate the deal if the buyer did not waive it. If the buyer waived their financing contingency per the 22AR, then if the buyer's financing fails (the loan does not fund) and the deal falls through, the earnest money deposit is typically not refundable to the buyer. You can still choose to refund it if you want but you are not usually legally required to do so. This kind of thing can happen and it is no fun for anyone involved. The buyers are usually devastated and you are completely upset because you have moved out of your house and now the deal is not going to go through. You need to be prepared in advance for this happening; i.e. at the beginning of this book your Plan B.

Keys and Cleaning...

You will need to arrange for your listing agent to collect all keys to your property so that on closing day she can deliver those to the buyer's agent once escrow notifies everyone that the deal is officially closed. Do not forget to include all copies of your keys, any mail box keys, garage door openers, shed or storage room keys. If you are in a condo, there may be a front door code you need to provide the buyer so they can enter the building or a fob, swipe card. Do not forget to fill out a change of address card with the post office. I suggest filling that out actually on closing day when you find out for sure the deal is really closing. Any mail that might get delivered to your old address during that forwarding gap can be collected for you by the buyer and you can pick it up or they can forward it to you.

Also, per the purchase and sale agreement you need to leave the property in the same condition it was in when it was listed; meaning that you clean it before you move out. If you are too stressed, then pay to have a cleaning service come in and clean the house once you have moved out. Take care to ensure the refrigerator/freezer is cleaned, bathrooms scrubbed, floors washed, carpets vacuumed, etc.... If you removed paintings from the walls, please make sure you remove the hanger hooks and spackle the holes, touch up the wall paint. Typically any window blinds need to remain with the property, as they are usually considered to be permanently attached. If you have a yard, remember to have it mowed or cleaned up as well, as you are also obligated to leave the grounds in the same condition they were in when you entered your purchase and sale agreement. You might also leave a simple gift welcoming the buyer and include a short note with any instructions or items about the property the buyer may need or want to know. You can also leave the appliance manuals with this as well. This keeps things friendly makes the buyer feel welcome.

If there is a yard sign with your listing, your agent should arrange to have that removed and that typically happens no later than a week after the closing date. Your agent will also be removing the key box from your property, either on closing day or shortly thereafter.

Real Life...

I had a buyer who was purchasing an upscale house that came with a custom designed kitchen. In the kitchen were custom cabinetry, a high end refrigerator that cost more than some people earn in a year and ditto for the restaurant grade range and oven. There were no notices posted at the house or anywhere in the listing paper work to indicate that the seller intended to take the appliances or replace them prior to moving out. The listing report indicated all of the appliances were included in the sale and that is what the purchase and sale agreement stated. Five days prior to closing, per the terms of the purchase and sale agreement, my client and I toured the house for his final walk through. The seller had already moved out and all was looking spic and span until we walked into the kitchen. The pricey refrigerator had been removed and in its place was a basic white refrigerator from Home Depot. Not only that, but this refrigerator did not fit flush within the custom designed cabinetry as the previous high end refrigerator had. Next, the million dollar range/oven was missing and a standard, four-burner, range/oven from Home Depot sat in its place. This too was dwarfed by empty space around it as the expensive range had at least eight burners and a grill and was considerably larger.

We took pictures and I immediately contacted the listing agent and escrow. The listing agent insisted that her seller was within his rights to remove the included appliances. She said the seller had replaced them with a like kind so everything was fine. I then contacted the listing agent's designated broker to let him know there was a problem. I sent over photos of the appliances that were currently in the kitchen and suggested they compare them with the photos of the kitchen's appliances that were posted with the listing online. After many calls, their stance was that the seller felt he was within his rights to remove the refrigerator and range/oven and felt his replacements were acceptable. I advised my client to postpone his signing appointment and consult with a local real estate attorney.

In the end, the seller had to restore the original appliances and allow us to re-inspect and then proceed to closing. Apparently the seller was furious with the listing agent for not informing him that he could not remove the appliances and replace them with cheaper substitutes. Even if he had replaced them with similar grade/style appliances, my buyer could have probably gone after him to put the original appliances back in the kitchen. If the seller had indicated per the listing paperwork and via the mutually signed purchase and sale agreement that the refrigerator and range/oven were not included with the sale, then this would have been a different situation.

It is frequently the details in real estate that make or break a smooth sale. In this case, the listing agent could have been clearer with her seller as to what he agreed to, via the listing paperwork and the signed around purchase and sale agreement. It meant he could not remove or replace the refrigerator or range. Still, there are cases where the listing agent is clear with her client, and the seller still decides to up and change the rules and terms without notifying anyone. Please do not be one of these kinds of sellers! Once you have a signed around deal you have a legal obligation to adhere to all of the terms you agreed to. You cannot randomly decide to change something or think you are going to get away with something, as clearly was the case in the example above. Doing something like this is not in your best interest and you will get caught. The resulting litigation or work you have to do to undo what you should not have done to begin with, is really not worth it.

NINE

LOOSE ENDS

Typical Players...

L et's sum up who the typical key players are in the home selling process.

1. <u>Buyer's Agent or Selling Agent</u>: The real estate agent who represents the buyer in the purchase of a property.

2. <u>Listing Agent</u>: The real estate agent who represents the seller in the sale of a property.

3. <u>Lender</u>: The institution or person who is loaning money to the buyer to purchase the home.

4. <u>Inspector</u>: The person the buyer selects and pays to inspect the property he is purchasing.

5. <u>Appraiser</u>: The person the lender's company contacts to go out and evaluate the subject property; i.e. make sure the loan is for a legitimate property and the sale price is of fair market value. The buyer pays for this, and the loan person will instruct when and how this payment is made. Note, loan officers are no longer allowed to cherry pick their appraisers. Appraisers are now randomly assigned to each property evaluation project.

6. <u>Title Company</u>: Usually selected by the seller when the property is first listed. They investigate the title for the subject property and make sure the title is clear and can be conveyed. The seller usually pays for this service.

7. <u>Escrow Company</u>: Buyer typically chooses this one. They are the third party referee who makes sure all money is disbursed properly and conditions to the purchase and sale agreement have been met. They ensure the deed is recorded by the county in the buyer's name. They notify all parties once the deed records and this is when the keys can be exchanged. The buyer and seller both pay for this service and it appears as a line item on your settlement statement. Note, sometimes (via your deal) you may agree to pay for the buyer's portion of the cost for this service.

There can be other entities involved but the above list is a good outline of who is usually involved in the home selling process.

A Good Listing Agent...

Here is a list of what I think a good listing agent is going to do.

1. Always puts your best interest first.
2. Educates you about the home selling process prior to listing your property.
3. Provides you with a sample purchase and sale agreement to review prior to listing, so you can become familiar with it, ask any questions in advance.
4. Provides you with an estimated seller's net proceeds sheet prior to listing your property so you are aware of the approximate total costs to sell the house at the given list price and the estimated amount you should net.
5. Provides you with a seller disclosure statement to fill out prior to your listing going live. Posts this completed form

with your listing, so interested buyers have easy access. Checks the form to ensure you have answered all required questions, provided explanations where necessary and properly initialed/signed and dated each page.

6. Makes sure you complete the most recent version of the seller disclosure statement and has you complete a new one if the form is updated or you discover a new material fact that has to be disclosed.

7. Explains title to you and helps you order preliminary title for your property prior to listing. Has you review and sign a legal description for your property (per WA State law) and posts that with your listing for easy access when a buyer wants to write up an offer on your property.

8. Does not always tell you what you want to hear.

9. Does not bad mouth you, the property or list price.

10. Refers you to a local real estate attorney (has a list for you to choose from) at any point during the selling process if legal advice or help is needed.

11. Fields all questions from prospective buyers and agents and answers questions about you or why you are selling per your specific instructions.

12. Does not pretend to know everything and will say, "*I don't know the answer, let me look into that and get back to you.*" If it is a question of a legal nature, your agent cannot answer it even if he knows for sure what the answer is. Hopefully in that case, he will do what item ten states.

13. Refers all loan questions, finance matters to the buyer's loan person.

14. Advises you speak with your tax advisor if you have questions related to how the profits from the sale of your property affects your tax bill.

15. Puts you in touch with a 1031 exchange facilitator company (if applicable) to explain to you how those transactions work and for you to learn more about how this type of transaction affects your annual taxes.

16. Ensures you get a complete copy of all paperwork, including everything you sign, either via email (with your permission) and/or hardcopy. You should receive copies of each form as you go, so you have it available, not get one big packet of all your paperwork on the day you close.

17. Does not guarantee that the property you are selling is going to make you money or guarantee any current or future conditions concerning the property.

18. Does not profess to be the neighborhood listing expert, know everything about an area and potential buyers. He may know a lot and may even live in the area but he should not put himself out there as your primary source for all information on a particular area. Legally, if questions are asked by a buyer about the area or your property you need to consult with the proper regulators on your own or with a local real estate attorney. Your agent can help you find the right agencies/authorities for information but legally your

agent should not be answering for those entities or relaying messages from them to you or the buyer.

19. Follows Federal Fair Housing Law; i.e. does not answer your questions about a potential buyer that are related to race, politics, religion, familial status, etc... or provide that kind of information regarding your neighborhood to any prospective buyers or their agents.

20. Puts in writing that she does not give or receive compensation for referrals; i.e. lenders, inspectors, service people. Collecting certain referral fees is illegal (it is illegal for an agent and a loan person to give one another any kind of consideration for a client referral). If a referral fee is not illegal, you most likely still do not want your agent collecting or giving referral fees to line her pocket and influence her referral selections.

21. Provide you with an Agent Detail and a Client Detail Report once your listing is live so you can see what agents and buyers actually are getting when they review your listing report via the MLS.

22. Helps you weigh the various pros and cons of the offer(s) you are looking at.

23. Does not do dual agency deals, only represents you the seller.

24. Does not poach other agents' clients; i.e. bad mouth other agents (either out right or in subtle passive aggressive ways)

and does not try to get other agents' clients to convert and work with them.

25. Remains grounded and helps you calm down if you become emotional.

26. Is organized, timely and polite.

27. Checks in with you at least once a week, even once your deal is in the hands of the buyer's loan person and you are in the countdown to closing phase.

28. Ensures that you have all repair work that you agree to do via your contract or inspection contingency taken care of prior to the buyer's final walk through date.

29. Forwards all receipts/invoices/warranties for any repair work you agree to do marked "paid-in-full" to the buyer's agent, the lender and to escrow.

30. Arranges to deliver all keys, fobs, door openers to the buyer's agent once escrow notifies everyone the deal is closed.

31. Maintains good records and paper trails all important communications involved in your transaction. You may see this as cc's on emails to other players in your deal or as an email that summarizes an earlier phone conversation.

A Good Seller...

In fairness, a seller needs to be aware of how their behavior affects the home selling process. Here is a list of some traits a good seller usually has.

1. Takes time up front to learn about the home selling process and organize things prior to listing.

2. Interviews agents and chooses the best match for them based not just on listing price but on competence and ability to organize and help you.

3. Reads through the sample purchase and sale agreement that their agent provides.

4. Reviews the provided estimated seller's net proceeds sheet and makes sure it is okay with them prior to listing.

5. Reads all listing paperwork and approves all marketing verbiage, photos.

6. Completes a seller disclosure statement (in full) prior to their listing going live so their agent can post this with the listing for easy access by interested buyers.

7. Pays the fee to open title for their property, reviews the preliminary title report and signs the legal description (per WA State law) so the agent can post that with the listing.

8. Takes responsibility for their sale and its inherent risks and rewards.

9. Contacts their home insurance representative prior to listing to inquire about any additional coverage which may be necessary while their house is listed.

10. Removes all prescription drugs, valuables, irreplaceable items from their home prior to listing or showings. Does not leave financial statements, credit cards, check books, cash, and jewelry lying around.

11. If their agent suggests speaking with a local real estate attorney, does so as soon as possible.

12. Removes or cages any pet prior to a showing per what you and your listing agent decided was best.

13. Listens to their agent's showing instructions and vacates the property whenever there is a showing or inspection.

14. When encountering buyers or agents is polite and does not engage in talk about the subject property, quiz the buyer or agent.

15. Refers all questions about their property, especially from any buyers or their agent, to the listing agent. Have your listing agent be your public buffer, that's what they are there for.

16. Instructs their listing agent as to how to answer such questions as, "*Why is the seller moving?*"

17. Does not blame their agent for poor showing feedback or for their house not selling fast enough. No listing agent has control over the state or speed of the current market. If your agent has done everything outlined and is competent, then there is really no magic solution they can provide to make your property sell faster.

18. Does not try and hide any flaws in their property; i.e. covering a damaged wood floor, a hole in the wall, etc...

19. Does not try and take or switch out any included appliances that your listing paperwork states remain with the property.

20. Does not lie or provide false information to anyone including their agent, the buyer's loan person, the title representative, escrow officer or the buyer.

21. Notifies their agent if a buyer's agent does not leave a business card, leaves a door open, does not follow the posted showing instructions, etc... so their agent can (hopefully) report them.

22. Does not allow random people who are not accompanied by a real estate agent to enter their home and tour it; i.e., *"We saw the for sale sign and would like to take a quick look at your house."* Tell them to have their agent contact your listing agent to arrange for a showing. It is not safe for you to allow a stranger to randomly enter your home, no matter how wholesome they may appear. Even a 75 year old grandma type could be scoping your place for her grandson who runs a robbery ring (true story). No serious home buyer is going to expect you to randomly let them in to see your house without an agent accompanying them. If someone who is with this would-be buyer says they are an agent, ask them for their business card. If the showing instructions require an appointment, tell them to make one per the MLS listing report's showing instructions. Let your listing agent know this agent's name so they can look them up and see if they are in fact a licensed agent and they can follow up with them later for a showing or feedback.

175

23. Reports anyone who asks them to falsify information or who they suspect are committing fraud to local professional boards and state oversight agencies.

24. Does not ask their agent to provide legal or tax advice or expect their agent to violate any licensing laws on their behalf.

25. Does not try and have their agent include personal property items in their purchase and sale agreement's paperwork and does not ask the agent to broker the sale or conveyance of personal items between the seller and buyer as a side transaction.

26. Is aware their agent has other clients who also require time, have scheduled appointments and does not expect their agent to drop everything to accommodate them.

27. Does not use social media to bad mouth the buyer or the deal; i.e. boast about what a great deal you just got and how dumb the buyers are, especially prior to closing. I advise my sellers to keep their mouths shut, and their social media addictions at bay until the deal has closed. Deals have literally imploded over a seller or buyer posting information about each other/the deal online.

28. Keeps their agent informed at all times of any day trips, out of town work/vacation commitments, etc.… Makes sure their agent knows how to reach them at all times until their deal is closed.

Seller's Remorse...

The more thought and organization you put into selling your home, the better your end result should be. Still, once you have accepted an offer and you are in a deal, you may get a case of the *"what ifs."* Also, like a swarm of locusts, everyone you know and their cousin Cindy are going to come out of the woodwork and offer their opinion on your sale and what they think about your deal. Please do not let these Monday morning real estate quarterbacks negatively influence you. What's that expression, *"opinions are like...?"* You will know you have done your prep work by reading this book and other research. You will know that you took the time to pick the best people available to work with. This is not something you did impulsively or without research. Turn the peanut gallery off! It amazes me how almost everyone you meet or know will offer you an unsolicited opinion on real estate. There are also those who are jealous or have some other kind of problem and who seem to thrive on casting doubt on your home sale. Most of these folks have watched way too much "reality" real estate TV shows. Please do not for a second believe those TV shows adequately show you what the home selling experience is like.

Another very important point, remember that once you have an offer you cannot randomly change your listing terms, suddenly raise the list price, decide you want to keep the appliances you previously indicated via your listing paperwork were included in the sale. The time for these types of changes was long ago and you are legally obligated to adhere to the posted terms of your listing and the agreed to terms in your deal.

CHARLES CHAPLIN
Blame Game, Victim...

I am astounded by the number of sellers that for years after their sale will blame their listing agent for some aspect of the sale. A while back I was at an open house and a looky-loo neighbor walked in. She enjoyed looking and then proceeded to vent about how awful her listing agent had been years ago when she sold. I did not know her agent but she ranted on and on about how her agent "made" her accept a bad offer and how she should have earned more money from that sale. Nothing I heard sounded to me like she had worked with a slimy agent. Rather I think she is a type of person that enjoys feeling they have been wronged. She went on and on about how her listing agent should have gotten her more money for her house. Given the time period she mentioned she sold, she should be thrilled she had a sale period. No listing agent no matter how good they are can manifest an awesome offer for you and make your property sell for the perfect price you are seeking. There is no magic crystal ball. Why spend your time dwelling on your sale and years bad mouthing your agent for something they ultimately have no control over? If you discover your agent was not so good or they are unethical, rather than blame them for years, move on, wise up and the next time make a more informed decision.

This unfortunately is par for the course for real estate agent stories that I hear at least every month or so. Many times it does not sound to me like the person telling the story had a bad or unethical agent. Rather, I think in some cases they are pissy people who want to blame someone else for their aggravations, their lack of money, happiness, etc…, and who better to project all of that on then the bad old real estate agent? Don't get me wrong, this profession is rife with sleaze balls and skanky agents. But there are also wonderful people who are real estate agents, who work hard, are honest and truly work in their client's best interest. So whining and blaming the real estate agent for not getting you enough money on the sale or not enough buyers toured your property, or the market was slow is in my opinion childish.

If you set up your sale and are organized like this book has shown you, then you can expect a better result. Becoming an informed home seller also means you need to accept responsibility for your actions and decisions. You need to be accountable and not blame others for the decisions you make or for not getting everything you think you deserve. You can go out and work with someone who is unethical, be an uninformed seller and as a consolation, you can then legitimately play the victim role and blame the shady agent for years to come. Or you can choose to be an informed seller and work with honest people. There is still some risk involved whenever you sell but at least you have done as much homework as you can to make an informed decision. You might not get everything you want but you are an informed and responsible seller, not a perpetual, whining, victim.

Fraud…

If you suspect anyone you are working with in the home selling process of committing fraud or perhaps you think what they are doing is not so ethical or a bit shady, then you should consider reporting it. You should first question them directly about whatever it is you think is problematic or not above board. If you still are not satisfied you can then escalate things.

If you believe your agent is not working on the up and up, and you have questioned them but are still not okay, then you should contact their designated broker or the owner of their brokerage. See what they have to say. Next, you could visit a real estate attorney, contact the local board of Realtors (if your agent is a member of NAR), contact the state licensing department's real estate division and there is always the state attorney general's office.

There are also the local media outlets with their consumer reporters, who are usually chomping at the bit to report a fraud story on a local entity. Just make sure you are not acting prematurely or flying off the handle and that what you are concerned about is legitimate. You need to have documentable evidence, not just "*he said/she said*" and you need to have given whomever you have a problem with ample time to respond to your query and concern.

Real Life...

One thing I have always been floored by is the number of listing agents who freely bad mouth their seller, the property or the list price. When I am representing a buyer, I contact the listing agent to let them know I have a buyer who is going to write up an offer on their listing. Without prompting sometimes I will hear how annoying the seller is and the listing agent cannot wait to unload this property and just to speed things along, they suggest that my buyers offer five thousand below the list price as the listing agent is pretty sure the seller will accept less. I always pass this information along to my buyers and sometimes if the comps show the list price is correct, then my buyer might still offer less per the listing agent's comment. Technically, I do not know if the seller instructed their listing agent to tell a potential buyer this or not. I highly doubt it but in reality who knows!

Another way this could come up is at an open house. The listing agent holds the house open on a Sunday while the seller is out. The listing agent tells potential buyers who are touring that she does not think the list price is accurate but the seller insisted. Or they might say you should consider writing up an offer for this place because they know (or think) you can get it for less. Again, these kinds of comments I do not always think are things the seller instructed their listing agent to freely share with potential buyers or their agents but who can say for sure. Incidentally, it's usually this type of listing agent who will also then tell the people touring their open house that she is happy to write up an offer for them and makes sure the seller gets it right away; i.e. she will be a dual agent.

I have a friend in another state who listed her house for sale a few years back. She chose someone to be her listing agent who she knew through her church and who was a very well known top producer agent. She thought this person was her friend and would represent her well. This agent listed her home and was there for the first open house. Out of the blue, my friend's coworker decided to stop by the open house and check things out. He had heard my friend talk about the work involved in listing her house and he was curious to see how her house looked now that is was on the market. He walked in the open house and was looking around when her listing agent descended

181

on him. Rather than let on as to who he really was and that he was not in the market to buy a house, he decided to play along with her agent. This listing agent proceeded to tell him what a pain the home owner (his coworker) was, how the list price was at least ten thousand more than it should be and if he had any interest, she would be happy to put in an offer for him and "work" on her seller. He continued to play along and gave the listing agent his contact information. She followed up that evening and again stated in her email to him that the list price was too high and she could get him a better deal. She also told him that the seller had let on that she would pay to have the whole house re-carpeted if a buyer ended up requesting that.

This is bad in many ways but bad and stupid joined together on this one! The listing agent incriminated herself via her email to the seller's co-worker. Long story short, the listing was terminated and my friend ended up suing the listing agent and her brokerage for defaming her and the property. It was eventually settled out of court. To my knowledge this listing agent got a slap on the wrist and is still in business selling real estate today. So again, please do your homework before you choose your listing agent and if you want, maybe send a "test monkey" over to see what actually happens when you are not around at an open house.

Final Word...

I hope this book is informative and helps you in your home selling quest. I did not state you would finish this book and be a real estate expert, nor did I say that my way (my opinions) are the only way. The goal is you are better informed about the whole home selling process having read this book. You now have the background needed to ask crucial questions and to recognize a red flag when you see one. If you found this book helpful, please recommend it to others. The companion book, <u>Home Buying for Smarties</u> is available for anyone you know who is considering buying a home. If you need a laugh and a light read, my satirical real estate mystery novels are also available, the titles are listed in the "About the Author" section as is my contact information. Here's to being an informed home buyer and enjoying life, cheers!

TEN

QUICK GLANCE

This chapter provides you with a quick reference guide and a book review quiz.

You Are Here...

Here is an outline of the basic steps to selling a property. It does not include any deal specifics or common variations.

1. Select your agent and review the listing agreement and estimated seller's net proceeds.

2. Choose the title company and have the preliminary title report pulled and legal description provided.

3. Complete a seller disclosure statement and sign the legal description (in WA State) to go with your listing.

4. Contact your home insurance company and let them know your house is going to be for sale, ask if there is any additional coverage you need while your home is listed.

5. Prepare your property for listing.

6. Select your list price based on the provided active and sold comp data and your estimated seller's net proceeds sheet.

7. Listing goes live, including any special showing instructions.

8. Receive an offer and review updated estimated seller's net proceeds.

9. Accept an offer and reach mutual agreement.

10. Vacate for the buyer's schedule inspection date/time.

11. Review buyer's inspection requests, if any. Review your revised estimated seller's net proceeds sheet accounting for any repairs you agree to pay for.

12. Agree to the buyer's inspection requests or not.

13. Buyer's lender orders the appraisal; vacate the property for the scheduled appraisal.

14. Review the title updates that the title company sends to you regarding the property you are selling.

15. Attend your scheduled signing appointment with escrow. Review the net gain on your settlement statement and compare it with your updated estimated seller's net proceeds. Those numbers should be fairly close.

16. Receive notification from escrow that the deed has recorded in the buyer's name and they are now the owner.

17. Your agent delivers all keys to the buyer's agent.

18. Thank your agent for helping you through this seemingly endless maze of obscure steps! If you truly like them, then refer them to your friends and family.

Loan Peeps...

Here is a basic list of the people who are involved in completing the buyer's loan and making sure your deal happens.

1. **Loan officer or mortgage broker**: the financial salesperson who the buyer chooses to work with, who assesses their financial situation and pre-approves them for a loan product to finance their property purchase. This is their primary money contact person throughout the home

buying odyssey and they keep the buyer updated as to their loan application's progress.

2. **Processor**: the person assigned to work with the buyer's loan officer/mortgage broker who organizes their file's paperwork and begins to execute the necessary steps to secure the buyer's loan.

3. **Underwriter**: the person within the buyer's loan person or mortgage broker's company who reviews their loan file and the signed around purchase and sale agreement. They ensure there are no outstanding conditions or issues with the buyer, their loan, or the property that the buyer is using their company's money to buy. This is the person escrow sends the buyer's signed loan documents to for final review and approval. They notify escrow on the closing day that the funds for the buyer's loan have been released.

4. **Appraiser**: the person who is contacted by the lender to complete the appraisal. The appraisal is the process by which the lender assesses the property the buyer is purchasing and makes sure the buyer is purchasing a viable property at a fair market price. The buyer pays for this, although in rare cases a buyer may request a seller pay for this.

Review Quiz...

1. Madeline receives a blank purchase and sale agreement from her real estate agent to review prior to listing her house. She has several specific legal questions about it and

a tax question. Is it okay for her agent to answer her legal questions? Is her agent the best person to answer tax questions?

2. Shalimar's cousin, Ricardo, just got his real estate license and wants to be her listing agent. Her boss knows a real estate agent, Jan, and he is constantly asking Shalimar if she is working with Jan yet. What should Shalimar consider telling her cousin and boss?

3. Cynthia has received an offer from a buyer for her house. Her listing agent tells her she might not want to accept this offer as she thinks the buyer is of a certain ethnic group or religion. What should Cynthia do?

4. Is the term "broker" something that should impress me?

5. Beth's listing agent tells her not to worry about the rotting deck located outside of her kitchen. She says she will make a note for buyers and agents not to walk on it. The listing agent says this repair can be passed along to buyer or taken care of later once there is an offer. Is this good advice?

6. Hank's listing agent says she is going to use a wide angle lens when photographing the rooms in his narrow, in-city townhouse. Is this a wise thing to do?

7. Your listing agent calls you and says she has great news, because she has found the perfect buyer for your house and they are going to write up an offer right away. What should you do?

8. Is it really that important that your listing agent post certain forms online with your listing when it goes live?

9. Your listing agent tells you that he will mention in the listing report verbiage that your property is being sold "as is" and this will greatly reduce your liability as a seller and/or mean you do not have to provide a seller disclosure statement to a buyer. Is this good information?

10. An agent you are interviewing to list your home, says she can guarantee that your will net X amount of dollars. Should this impress you?

11. When should a listing agent be providing you with an estimated seller's net proceeds sheet?

12. Sally's listing agent told her there is no need for her to pay for a new Resale Certificate or the CC&Rs with her condo sale. This agent says she has a copy of these forms from a sale she just did with another listing in the condo complex. She says she can white out certain information and Sally can use this to provide to a buyer and save herself the money and bother of ordering a Resale Certificate and CC&Rs. Is this a good bonus and a reason Sally should choose to work with this listing agent?

13. Bill had a signed around deal for his house. The buyers did their inspection and their inspector found quite a few items that needed to be repaired. Via their inspection response, the buyer's submitted to Bill a long list of items they wanted repaired and backed it up with the pertinent pages

from their home inspector's inspection report. Bill reviewed the requested items and the home inspection report data but decided against repairing the items. The buyers decided to terminate the deal and buy something else. Bill's listing agent tells him there is no real need for him to redo his seller disclosure statement, since she is not going to tell anyone what the previous buyer's inspector found wrong and there's really no chance of this information getting out. What should Bill do?

Quiz Answers...

1. It is never okay for Madeline's real estate agent to answer her legal questions. All legal questions must be referred to a local real estate attorney. Her agent is also not the person to ask about tax related questions. Madeline should consult with a tax professional. Go to the appropriate sources to get the best information and results.

2. Shalimar should politely tell everyone that this is business first, nothing personal. She will make up her own mind as to those she chooses to represent her/work with her. She is not going to be pressured or manipulated by others into working with people she does not fully investigate and believe are a good match for her.

3. Cynthia should report this listing agent for violating the Federal Fair Housing Law. No real estate agent is permitted to tell you that an offer is good or bad depending on the buyer's ethnicity, religion, familial status, etc....

4. The generic term "broker" should not impress you. In WA State, that term is used to refer to any person who has a real estate license. Regardless of where you live, remember to investigate terms, designations, and awards that any agent or loan person touts and find out firsthand exactly what they mean before you are blindly impressed.

5. This is bad advice and Beth should find a new agent. Repair work large and small should be done to your property prior to listing to ensure your property shows as good as it can and that buyers do not fixate on the items that need repairing while they are touring. This will help you get the best offer from a potential buyer. Repair items like a rotting deck can also be a seller liability issue even if your agent notes in the listing report that people touring your house should not walk on the deck.

6. No. Using wide angle lenses to photograph rooms does not serve you well. Most people looking at the photos online can tell that type of lens has been used and when a buyer tours the property and finds the rooms are narrower than the posted photographs led them to believe they will not be happy. It can also cause the buyer to start to wonder if the seller is doing something else that is manipulative or hiding something.

7. Politely tell your listing agent no and remind her that you do not want to participate in a dual agent deal. Your agent (in my opinion) needs to represent you alone not the buyer

of your property too. Hopefully, you will not encounter this situation as you weeded out any agents who do dual agency in your listing agent interview process.

8. Yes, posting forms online with your listing is crucial. Your agent should have had preliminary title ordered and if required in your state, you should have reviewed and signed the legal description. That should be posted with your listing so when a buyer wants to write up an offer, it is easily accessible and their agent can get them to sign it and include it with their offer paper work. You do not have mutual agreement (in WA State) until both parties have initialed the legal description. Deals have literally fallen part due to the legal description not being mutually acknowledged by both the seller and buyer. Your agent should also post your fully completed seller disclosure statement so the buyer can review and sign off on the last page and submit that with their offer as well. If your house was built prior to 1978, a lead disclosure form should also be signed by you and your agent and that form posted with your listing as well. Last, your agent needs to post with the MLS any letters on file which states offer terms you want a prospective buyer to follow, showing instructions, etc... This is not difficult it just requires that your agent is informed and organized.

9. Fire this agent right away! Indicating a, *"property is sold as is"* in your listing report remarks does not remove your

potential liability as a seller. Nor does it mean you are not required to provide a prospective buyer with the seller disclosure statement (in WA State).

10. No. If anything, any listing agent that says they will guarantee you a certain net return for your home's sale should not impress you, it should let you know not to hire this agent. Clearly this agent is clueless or a manipulator. No agent has any way to "guarantee" a seller a specific monetary net gain. They might say it is likely that you will net X amount but guarantee it, no.

11. At a minimum, a listing agent should provide you with an estimated seller's net proceeds sheet to you prior to deciding what your list price is going to be. I also think you should review an updated one before you sign off on any offer you receive and again when you are reviewing any repair requests a buyer may make via their inspection contingency. The final time to review it is when you are at your signing appointment at escrow.

12. No this is horrible and Sally needs to run. What this agent is proposing is illegal and could get Sally in a world of trouble down the line if it is discovered. A new Resale Certificate has to be provided to each buyer as well as the CC&Rs information. Yes, it is a pain to order these documents as most condominium management companies are not user friendly with this process at all and yes they are overpriced in my opinion. Regardless, the seller has a legal

obligation to provide this to a buyer and providing copies of an old version or an unofficial or altered copy could very easily result in legal action against you the seller. Do not do this and do not work with or hire any agent who touts being able to provide this illegal service to you as a bonus to you agreeing to list with them.

13. Bill should first fire his agent and then report her to the local MLS, local association of Realtors (if she is a member) and to the state's real estate licensing division. What she is advising is illegal and potentially puts him at great risk as a seller. Bill needs to fill out a new and revised seller disclosure statement which includes the new information he now has about his house as a result of the former buyer's home inspection. If Bill is unclear as to how this needs to be done or has questions, he should immediately consult with a local real estate attorney to assist him with updating the seller disclosure form. I always advise my sellers, if they have any doubts as to what to include or not include on this disclosure statement to consult with an attorney and if in doubt it is most likely in your best interest to go ahead and disclose everything you know about your property to avoid future troubles.

GLOSSARY
(Written from a seller's perspective)

ASHI: American Society of Home Inspectors.

Appraisal: the independent valuation of the property you are buying. This is ordered by the buyer's lender and is required for their loan to fund. Appraisers are no longer cherry picked or assigned to lenders; it is now a lottery assignment system. The **Appraiser** is the licensed person who actually goes out in the field and evaluates the property. This typically happens after the removal of the buyer's inspection contingency. The buyer usually pays for their appraisal.

As Is: a term typically used to indicate the property is being sold in its current condition and the seller is not open to addressing any repairs a buyer may want taken care of prior to closing. It is a term that is sometimes mistakenly used to indicate that the seller assumes no legal responsibility for the condition of the property and/or the seller will not provide a seller disclosure statement, even when required by law.

Bank Owned: a term used to describe a property that has been foreclosed on and is now for sale by the lien holder, bank. These properties are notorious for not being well maintained.

CC&Rs: the Covenants, Conditions, and Regulations for a condominium or co-op. Usually this is delivered with the Resale Certificate or the Public Offering Statement for the buyer to review.

Cash Offer: an offer on a property that is made without a financing contingency or lender involved. The buyer intends to pay for the property using cash, not a loan.

Closing: the date you and the buyer agree upon, via the purchase and sale agreement, to finalize the deal and convey title from the seller to the buyer and record the deed in the buyer's name. All purchase and sale agreements must have a clearly stated closing date in order to be valid and enforceable. Writing in "*to be determined*" in the closing date blank is not acceptable. Closing will not occur on a legal holiday, Saturday or Sunday.

Comparison Reports: the statistical reports for active and sold properties that are similar to your property within a local radius. Any member of your local MLS should be able to run these reports for you prior to listing your property and update them when you receive an offer. Also referred to as a **CMA, Comparative Market Analysis** or **Comps**.

Condominium: a shared housing complex whereby you own your actual unit and have common shared areas that are jointly owned and maintained by the homeowner's association. There are monthly or annual homeowner dues and all owners must abide by the CC&Rs.

Co-op: (**cooperative**) a shared housing complex where you own stock (shares) in the controlling corporation that actually owns all of the units. Your shares in the corporation are usually determined via the square footage and floor level of your particular apartment. There are monthly or annual homeowner dues and all owners must abide by the CC&Rs. All sales of apartments must be approved by the co-op board before interest can be assigned and shares issued. It is harder for a buyer to obtain financing for a co-op as opposed to a condominium.

Counter Offer: when a named party makes a change to an offer or rejects it outright and creates a new offer. Example, the buyer offers $320,000 and the seller counter offers back for $330,000. Then the buyer counters the seller's counter offer at $325,000, etc....

Current State of the Market: a phrase used to describe the housing market's condition; i.e. is it a seller's market or a buyer's market? Are sales fast or slow? Usually it shows how things are trending overall in a region or area. Note, there are micro market conditions; i.e. a specific neighborhood or price point may be moving fast but the rest of the market is very slow and not selling.

Deed: the written document that conveys the title to real property from the seller to the buyer. Escrow makes sure the appropriate county records this document and then notifies all parties the deal is closed and keys can be given out.

Dual Agent: an agent who represents both the buyer and seller in the sale of a property and is paid both the selling and listing office commissions for doing so. This is illegal in some states and in other states you the seller and the buyer have to agree in writing first before this can occur.

Earnest Money Deposit: (EMD) the amount of money the buyer pledges when making an offer to let the seller know they are serious about following through on their offer. This is usually tendered via a hard copy check or by an **Earnest Money Promissory Note** (a legally binding instrument that essentially substitutes for a check) when making the offer.

Easement: the right usually noted in your title report which gives, for example, the utility company permission to access the subject property to maintain their equipment, power lines, water pipes, etc.... Another common example is where the common driveway that crosses the subject property is noted and it is fully accessible to all parties which use it for ingress and egress to their adjoining properties. There are many forms of easements (implied, in gross, necessity) you can research or ask your title representative about these.

Escalation Addendum: an addendum to a buyer's offer that spells out how much over the offered price the buyer is willing to go in order to beat any competing offers. Usually escalation increments start at $1,000 and are used in multiple offer situations.

Escrow: the process where something of value is held by a neutral third party until contractual conditions have been met. This would be the buyer's earnest money deposit being held by the **Escrow Agent** (the escrow company) and later disbursed per the terms of the purchase and sale agreement and the buyer's loan officer's instructions. The escrow agent is usually selected when you are negotiating with a buyer. The **Escrow Officer** is a licensed person who works for the escrow agent (company). The escrow officer prepares your settlement statement per the buyer's lender and the purchase and sale agreement's instructions and ensures all money is paid and applied where indicated. Escrow ensures, once the buyer's funds are released by their lender that the title is conveyed and the deed is recorded in the buyer's name. Escrow notifies all parties once the deed is recorded in the buyer's name. The escrow fee is usually split equally between the seller and buyer but sometimes the buyer negotiates the seller paying his half of the escrow fee. Escrow issues the seller a check or wires the money to their account for their net gain on the sale after the deal closes. Escrow ensures the mortgages are paid off, commissions are paid to the listing and selling offices, all fees are deducted and taxes are paid, prior to issuing you your seller's net proceeds check.

Estimated Seller Net Proceeds: the data sheet your agent should give you prior to listing your property that outlines the various fees that you will be responsible for paying including commissions, estimated closing fees, taxes. Usually this can be represented as a percentage that you then multiply by the suggested list price. For example, suggested list price is $300,000 the estimated costs are approximately 9%, thus the estimated costs for listing and selling equals $27,000. If you accept an offer of $300,000 then your estimated seller gross is $273,000; your net is that amount less your mortgage. This sheet should be updated by your agent when you get an offer and revised again after the buyer's inspection, if they ask you to pay for any repair work in that phase. No one can guarantee exactly what your final net will be but you can have a very good estimation that is close to what your actual net ends up being.

Equity: the value you have in your property above the amount you owe on the property. Example, if your mortgage amount is $150,000 and your property's current market value (what you can get selling it today) is $320,000, then your equity is $170,000 (less selling fees and taxes). **Negative Equity**, is the economists polite way of saying you are losing money; i.e. your loan amount is $150,000 and your property's current market value is $100,000, thus you are $50,000 in the red.

Fair Market Value: the price or value that a specific property is worth based on market conditions at that point in time. Sometimes described as **what the market will bear**, the **market rate,** or the **going price**.

Financing Addendum: the part of a buyer's offer that outlines the buyer's specific loan conditions and timelines necessary for the buyer to secure their financing and complete the purchase.

Flipping: a term used when someone purchases a property that is in need of cosmetic upgrades and repair and they quickly fix it up in hopes of reselling it at a higher price and for a profit.

Foreclosure: when a lien holder (bank) evicts the mortgagor (home owner) who has defaulted on their home loan and takes back possession of the property. They usually then sell it in order to fully or partially satisfy the lien (loan). Foreclosed properties are also referred to as **bank owned**.

199

Full Service Agent: a traditional full time real estate agent who works with his clients from the very start of their home selling process all the way until closing and then follows up for years thereafter. This is in contrast to other business models where the seller is passed off to different people during the home selling process, the agent only works part time, or the seller pays flat rate fees for a company to list their property with the MLS and then does all the work themselves.

Home Buyer Warranty: a form of insurance or warranty a buyer or seller may purchase to cover stated items/systems in the subject property for a certain period of time after a transaction closes. Most usually cover the basic systems in a house; the furnace, appliances.

Home Owners Association: a group of home owners with a common or shared interest in a condominium, co-op or neighborhood. Members usually must pay monthly or annual monetary dues and are allotted voting powers for common projects and special assessments. The association usually elects a board to help manage the association and run things.

Home Owners Insurance: insurance a buyer pays for to cover the specific property he is buying. For a house it will cover the house itself and the lot it sits on. For a condominium it will cover the inside of the unit itself and usually a separate storage unit if applicable. Lenders require buyers purchase this, as do condominium home owner associations. Those purchasing a single family house with cash are strongly encouraged to purchase this form of insurance too. This is the company a seller should contact prior to listing their house, to make sure no additional coverage is needed while their house is listed for sale.

Inspection Contingency: the clause or form that makes a buyer's offer contingent upon a specified inspection time period, typically a week after the mutual acceptance date. During this time, a buyer may personally inspect the property and/or hire professional inspectors to look at it as well.

Law of Real Estate Agency: a pamphlet that is required in WA State to be given to all buyers and sellers of real estate. It describes a consumer's legal rights when dealing with a real estate broker in WA State.

Legal Description: the description of the property you are selling stated in legal terms. This verbiage is provided by the title company and in some states is required to be mutually acknowledged by both parties and included in the purchase and sale agreement paperwork in order for mutual acceptance to occur.

Lead Disclosure: a Federal booklet which explains the dangers of lead based paints and how this comes into play when selling a property. It is mandatory that this booklet be given to all home buyers and sellers. If a property was built prior to 1978 (the year lead in paint was banned in the United States), then a lead disclosure addendum needs to be included in the purchase and sale agreement and acknowledged by the seller, listing agent, the buyer, and the buyer's agent.

Letter on File: the written consent to certain listing conditions that your agent has you agree to and posts online with your property's listing per the rules and regulations of their local MLS. An example would be if you do not want showings between certain hours or you want to look at all offers, if any, on a specific date and time, or you will only review offers from buyers who are pre-approved for a loan, etc....

MLS: the Multiple Listing Service. This is the most common listing service in the United States that the majority of real estate agents belong to. It is membership based, meaning agents pay annual dues to be a member to their local affiliate and they must abide by member rules and regulations as stipulated by the MLS. The MLS is a vast, organized database of local or regional listings. The MLS is where most agents post their listings and buyer's agents go to search for available listings and check a property's status. The MLS is where most independent real estate websites around the country pull listings from to post on their sites. Each state or region within a state typically has its own MLS or listing organization. For example, in western Washington State it is the Northwest Multiple Listing Service (**NWMLS**).

Mortgagee: the party that lends the buyer money to purchase a property (the lending institution).

Mortgagor: the party that takes out the loan to purchase a property (the buyer).

Multiple Offers: when a property for sale is soliciting or has more than one offer being made on it at one time. A specific date and time are usually given for offer submissions in a multiple offer situation. A buyer may ask to do a pre-inspection on the property if they are going to waive their inspection contingency as part of their multiple offer strategy. Usually these offers will include an escalation addendum or sometimes you the seller may state you only want their best offer, no escalation addendums.

Mutual Acceptance: the term used to describe when a buyer and seller have come to a complete or a mutual meeting of the minds and all of the terms of a deal are agreed upon. This is also referred to as **Mutual Agreement**. This is when the buyer's offer has been fully accepted by the seller and from this point the timelines in the purchase and sale agreement activate and the clock starts ticking.

NAR: the National Association of Realtors, founded in 1908. Real estate agents who are members are called Realtors (a trademarked term) and are bound by the organization's Code of Ethics.

Neighborhood Review: the time period a buyer has to review a neighborhood or area where she is purchasing a home. The Inspection Contingency Form 35 (WA State) allows for a buyer to request a neighborhood review and then usually have three days after mutual acceptance is reached to review the neighborhood and terminate the transaction should they not like what they find.

Personal Property: items that are not permanently attached to the land or house. Examples: bird bath, freestanding bookshelf units, sofa, washing machine (if not noted as an appliance that stays in the listing report). The seller takes these items with him when he moves, unless there is a separate written agreement between the buyer and the seller regarding these types of items (which agents should not assist with or be a part of).

Pre-Approval: a certificate or letter provided by a buyer's lender which states that a buyer has been pre-approved for a loan (mortgage). It usually states the buyer's name, purchase price, loan amount, loan to value ratio, loan type(s), the term of the loan (i.e. 20 years), funds needed to close, any special conditions, the loan person's name and company name. The purchase price indicated on the initial pre-approval form is not always the amount a buyer wants to spend. It merely shows the maximum amount a buyer can spend based on his loan pre-approval. A buyer's pre-approval certificate or letter should always be updated to reflect the specific monetary conditions and amounts in her offer. It is usually valid for a few months after it is issued. It is not a commitment to lend but it does show that a buyer has met with the loan person and they have most likely run credit, reviewed numbers, talked about various loans that are available and verified certain lending conditions are met. A wise listing agent is going to require a copy of a buyer's loan pre-approval be submitted with their offer (per seller instructions/letter on file).

204

Purchase and Sale Agreement: (**PSA**) the documents that are used to create an offer to purchase your property. The PSA is the enforceable agreement or contract that the buyer and the seller have both fully acknowledged. It details the terms, conditions and timelines the buyer and the seller are working under for the sale of the property. This can also be referred to as your **Agreement**, **Contract**, **Deal**, **Transaction**.

Real Estate Agent: a term used to describe anyone who is licensed to sell real estate. Also commonly referred to as an **Agent**, **Salesperson**, **Broker**.

Real Property: a term used to describe the land and/or anything permanently attached to it. Example, a lot with a ranch style house built on it or a lot with a condominium complex built on it.

Realtor: a person who is licensed to sell real estate and is also a member of the National Association of Realtors. The Association trademarked this term in 1949. Pronounced "real"+ "tor"—there is no "i" in the middle.

Resale Certificate: the document a buyer receives when purchasing an existing (not new construction) condominium or co-op. It usually states the monthly dues, gives ownership ratios, financial reserves, and indicates if there is pending litigation against the homeowner's association. The CC&Rs are usually delivered with this certificate for the buyer to review. In WA State, a buyer has five days after receipt to review the Resale Certificate, ask questions and/or terminate the deal based on this review. This is also sometimes called the **Resale**. The seller has to order and pay for this paperwork once an offer is accepted and the usual cost is between $300 and $500. A good listing agent is going to have their seller review this with their condominium's management company prior to listing so everyone is aware of the costs and expected turn-around time to receive and deliver these required documents to a buyer.

Rescission: the termination of a deal by both of the parties involved. Usually acknowledged by both parties in writing via a specific form depending on the legal reason the parties are terminating the deal.

Seller Disclosure Statement: the form that is required in some states for sellers to fill out and provide to a buyer that states certain known conditions or knowledge a seller may have about the property they are selling. In the NWMLS this form is commonly called the **Form 17**.

Settlement Statement: the final tally sheet that escrow puts together outlining all credits and debits for the buyer and seller and disbursements. As a seller, you will only see your side of this tally and will want to verify the numbers are accurate in accordance with your updated estimated seller's net proceeds sheet. The review of this statement occurs at your signing appointment. Once fully executed, this statement is also sometimes referred to as the **Final HUD**.

Short Sale: when the owner of a property does not have enough money to pay off their existing mortgage upon the sale of their property. The shortage of funds has to be negotiated by the seller and the lender (mortgage note holder).

Signing Appointment: the appointment you will attend to review the settlement statement and verify all debits are accurate and being paid and how credits are to be disbursed to you upon closing. This appointment is set up by escrow and they will let you know what form of photo identification and any funds you need to bring with you. In escrow states, your signing appointment is separate from the buyer's signing appointment and there usually are a few days after signing until closing takes place. In traditional settlement states, you have a concurrent signing appointment with the buyer and the deal closes the same day.

Title: the legal ownership of real property. Usually it is indicated by the filed written document called the deed.

Title Insurance: protects against future losses occurring as a result of past events. The seller pays for the title company to guarantee clear title for the property they are selling. A lender typically requires a buyer pay for a title insurance premium so as to protect their interest in the property they are loaning money on to purchase. Cash buyers are encouraged to purchase this insurance as an owner's policy.

Title Report: a document compiled by the chosen title company which details the condition of the title to a specific piece of property. A preliminary title report is usually pulled when a listing agent first takes a listing. Once a deal is signed around, the title company works on and issues the title report and updates it as necessary until the deal closes.

ABOUT THE AUTHOR

Charles Chaplin is a Managing Broker and was originally licensed in 1991 in Washington, DC. Charles has been selling real estate in the greater Seattle metro area since 1997. Since 2004, Charles has volunteered to teach hundreds of state certified home buyer classes. He is a certified clock hour instructor and a certified state bond program instructor. Charles is a multi-year Five Star Agent Award winner for *Seattle Magazine* and *Portland Monthly*. He has a B.A. in Economics and Communications.

If you need help with buying or selling a home in the greater Seattle metro area, or you need an agent referral for your part of the country, or you are an agent who would like information to join Charles' agent referral network, please reference this book's title in the subject header and send an email to Charles@lifeinseattle.com.

www.ingramcontent.com/pod-product-compliance
Lightning Source LLC
Chambersburg PA
CBHW070519200326
41519CB00013B/2849